PRAISE FOR
*From Ironing Board to Corporate Board*

"Ginny's journey isn't just a simple affirmation of the traditional values of growing up in a Chinese laundry, but a perceptive account of American life with all its opportunities, complexities, and injustices yet to be corrected. An immigrant child, a beauty queen, a teacher, a corporate board member, a talk show host, and a national president of one of the oldest civil rights advocacy groups in Washington D.C. are just some of the roles Ginny has played while pursuing her Asian American dreams."
—**Gary Mar**, Director, Asian American Center, Stony Brook University

"This modest memoir is a gem of an introduction to the lives of Chinese Americans, including hard-working immigrant parents and their children. Ginny describes her experiences as a young girl, growing up in a Chinese laundry, negotiating the intricate paths towards independence within a traditional family and the difficulties and joys of engaging the outside world."
—**Franklin Odo**, Director, Smithsonian Institute, Asian Pacific American Program

"In this wonderful autobiography, Ginny demonstrates how she came to be the person that she is – confident and strong, warm and personable, proud of her Chinese and Asian heritage, and committed to social justice for all. Going back to her childhood and her subsequent years growing up as a young Chinese American, Ginny integrates personal biography and social history seamlessly through delightful storytelling and personal reflection. I highly recommend the book to young Asian Americans who wish to compare their experiences 'growing up Asian American' with their family experiences."
—**Larry Hajime Shinagawa, PhD**, Director and Associate Professor, Asian American Studies Program, University of Maryland, College Park

"Ginny's story is my story. I can relate very well to it because we, like thousands of other Chinese immigrant families, grew up in laundries where we experienced hard work and long hours. From those humble roots we experienced the disparity of merging two cultures and being accepted by the dominant society. This book is a beacon to all immigrant youngsters confronting the same problems that we experienced growing up and adjusting to two societies."
—**Betty Lee Sung**, author, and professor at City University of New York

"This is a delightful story of a Chinese American girl of the '1.5 generation.' She is the thread that holds together the diverse patchwork of America. Born in

the Old World and arriving in the New at an early age, she is adept at navigating around the shoals of cultural anomalies. Because of her, the Chinese laundry shop immigrants, who are her parents, are able to make this alien land their home."
—**Veronica Li**, author of *Journey Across the Four Seas: A Chinese Woman's Search for Home*

"As a child of the Chinese hand laundry, I applaud Ginny's success going from ironing board to the corporate board, making community service a major part of her life work, and keeping in touch with the heart and soul of her life. Her story has brought back memories of my past, growing up behind a hand laundry in Brooklyn, New York. The future always looks and feels strong when it is filled with warm memories."
—**Laura Chin**, Former Executive Director, Organization of Chinese Americans

"I truly enjoyed reading Ginny's narrative of her coming into her own. I was struck by its clear, simple flow and yet complexity of the choices she made and the challenges she finessed, one at a time, to become the leader and multi-talented individual and model she is. In a time when many seem to have forgotten the fundamental steps of life that lead to lasting success, and it doesn't matter whether your origins are Asian, African, White, Hispanic, or Native American, Ginny has provided an excellent resource for secondary students – a modern 'Pilgrims' Progress' of how to arise from humble origins to pinnacles of success within the

American promise and dream of the right to the pursuit of happiness. She does so concisely, illustratively, and effectively. If you care for your children, you must read this book and make sure they read it too ... perhaps together."
—**William Poy Lee**, author of *The Eighth Promise*

"As one of Ginny's closest friends and just when I thought I knew everything about her and her family, she had taught and delighted me with new stories and wisdom with this wonderful work. It is a must read for young adults, family historians and Asian Americans to learn about our heritage."
—**Sandra Lee Kawano**, Past Chair, Chinatown Health Clinic, New York

"This book is more than just a story about a young girl's journey into adulthood. It is a powerful and honest account of an American heroine's negotiations through life as a perpetual foreigner; the lessons learned about character and nobility, respect and traditions."
—**Michael C. Lin**, Past National President, Executive Director of Organization of Chinese Americans (OCA), and Vice Chair of the Board of Trustees of Montgomery College

# FROM IRONING BOARD
# TO CORPORATE BOARD

# FROM IRONING BOARD
# TO CORPORATE BOARD

## My Chinese Laundry
## Experience in America

GINNY GONG

**Homa & Sekey Books**
**Paramus, New Jersey**

Library of Congress Cataloging-in-Publication Data

Gong, Ginny, 1948-

From ironing board to corporate board : my Chinese laundry experience in America / Ginny Gong Homa Sekey Books. — 1st ed. p. cm.

ISBN 978-1-931907-50-7 (pbk.)

1. Gong, Ginny, 1948- 2. Chinese Americans—Biography. 3. Gong, Ginny, 1948—Childhood and youth. 4. Gong, Ginny, 1948—Family. 5. Chinese Americans—New York (State)—Long Island—Biography. 6. Immigrants—New York (State)—Long Island—Biography. 7. First-born children—New York (State)—Long Island—Biography. 8. Laundries—New York (State)—Long Island—History—20th century. 9. Long Island (N.Y.)—Biography. 10. Long Island (N.Y.)—Ethnic relations. I. Title.

E184.C5G65 2008

973'.04951—dc22

2008025485

Homa & Sekey Books
3rd Floor, North Tower
Mack-Cali Center III
140 E. Ridgewood Avenue
Paramus, NJ 07652

Tel: 201-261-8810; 800-870-HOMA
Fax: 201-261-8890; 201-384-6055
Email: info@homabooks.com
Website: www.homabooks.com

Printed in U.S.A.
1 3 5 7 9 10 8 6 4 2

This book is dedicated to the "1.5" generation of Chinese Americans who grew up and learned the essential lessons of life in the back of a Chinese laundry. It is dedicated to the memory of my sister Florence, to my parents, Bing Kuey and Oy Jee, who made the laundry their life, to my brother, Ken, who was my childhood companion, and to my children, Jennifer, Brian, and David, who have been the sources of my inspiration to tell this story.

# CONTENTS

# FOREWORD I

That America's vitality lies in its immigrant history is a venerated belief of our nation. We have shining images of a welcoming Statue of Liberty. Pictures of ambitious new arrivals seeking new opportunities in a new land have become iconic American portraits. We proudly call ourselves descendants of immigrants. We celebrate our immigrant heritage as the source of the vigor and richness of America.

A little known aspect of that history, however, is the story of the people that traveled east across the Pacific Ocean to America. It is the story of the immigrants from Asia. They too came to this country with the classic immigrant dream of making a better life for themselves. Their experiences, however, were often far different from what they expected.

The first immigrant group from Asia to come to America was from China. It began as early as the middle of the 19th century. The Chinese called this new land of their hopes "Gold Mountain." The people from Japan began arriving in the latter part of that century. Immigration from Korea had just begun around the beginning of the 20th century when it was quickly restricted in 1907. From the very outset, immigrants from Asia were harshly received.

All immigrants to America could someday aspire to become a naturalized citizen of the United States, all, – except those that came from Asia. From the very time of their arrival, Asians were singled out. Asian immigrants were denied naturalization simply because they were Asian. They were forbidden land ownership in the United States. They were denied the protection of the law of the land. In fact, there were countless discriminatory laws passed against them. Indeed, the door on any further immigration from China was slammed shut in 1882 and from Japan in 1924. It wasn't until after the middle of the 20th century that entry was relaxed for immigrants from Asia.

The early immigrants from Asian countries – China, Japan and Korea – came to America fleeing the turbulence of each of their own nations back home, bringing with them their own language and culture, and each with their own national prejudices against each other. However, once in the United States, they were treated collectively as Asians, legislated against as Asians, and experienced life in America as Asians. Whether from China, Japan, or Korea, the early immigrants from Asia shared the same struggles, similar challenges and each had to demonstrate like resilience. They lived through a common American experience as Asians. However, when their American born children grew up sharing a common language – English – they became Asian Americans. They became people with a common American background.

This is the large tapestry that is the backdrop to the story of Ginny Gong. She and her family were mid 20th century arrivals when their plane landed at Idyllwild Airport in New York in 1954. The America they encountered had been changed by wars in Asia. Some Americans who had served in the military in Asia had married Asian women. Some Asian Americans were now entering various professions. The harsh discrimination encountered by the early immigrants from Asia had moderated, but they were far from gone. There were still the hurdles of language, culture, and racial bias. It took determination and sacrifice on the part of Ginny's parents to build their lives in the new land. It took talent and spirit by Ginny to build her life as an Asian American.

Ginny's journey from the ironing board of a Chinese hand laundry to corporate boards and public service is a story of transformations. It is not only the advance of an immigrant girl from China into a dynamic Asian American public servant. It is also the transformation of a nation from one with only show-case principles to becoming one with living, breathing ideals. America today is a better, truer democracy and activists have been the vital catalyst in that transformative process. Ginny the activist is a vibrant creation as well as a creator of the work-in-progress that is our Democracy. She is the embodiment of the American dream come real.

George Takei
Actor, Activist
Mr. Sulu in *Star Trek*

# FOREWORD II

It's been delightful to spend a quiet afternoon on the Labor Day weekend reading and reflecting on Ginny's excellent book that describes her own experience growing up in a Chinese immigrant family. As a child of first generation immigrants, Ginny recounts her life from the time she arrived in the U.S. with her mother and younger brother to join her father in 1954 when she was only six years old. From there her personal experiences as a new immigrant began to unfold. Even though the book was written for young adult readers, as a first generation immigrant myself, I was deeply moved by her fascinating experiences and enjoyed very much reading of her struggles to grow up in a country about which she knew almost nothing when she first stepped out of the plane. Ginny described many of the cultural clashes that she experienced and how she made the best adjustments eloquently.

Although every immigrant may have a different background and encounters different obstacles, they learn to love their newly adopted country, wanting to become a good citizen by working hard and making the best adjustment possible. Ginny's life story and her eventual success is one of the best examples. I recommend this book not only to the young readers who are interested in learning about the experiences of immigrants but also to those who study the history of immigration. America is a country of immigrants. The history of immigration is therefore a very important part of American history. In recent years, we have seen the fast expansion of Asian American studies in American universities. Ginny's book represents a good case study for Asian American studies and for the study of American immigration history. It deserves a place in every library and personal reading list.

Serving her fourth term as the National President of the Organization of Chinese Americans (OCA), a national pan-Asian American organization, Ginny has excelled as a national leader dedicated to advancing the *social, political,* and *economic well-being* of all Asian Pacific Americans. Her long journey moving from the ironing board to the corporate board serves as an inspiration for us all.


Hwa-Wei Lee, PhD
Chief of Asian Division, the Library of Congress
Dean Emeritus of Ohio University Libraries
September 3, 2007

# ACKNOWLEDGEMENTS

I am truly grateful to so many people for their encouragement and support of this project over the years. Thanks to my dear friend, Michael Lin, for his unconditional support of this and many of my projects, to Cindy Tong and Aryani Ong for being wonderful resources, to George Takei and Hwa-Wei Lee for so eloquently creating the framework in the forewords, to Veronica Li, William Po Lee and Gary Mar for their initial constructive suggestions, and to Laura Chin, Sandra Kawano, Fred Quan, Bill Ng, Virginia Ng, Franklin Odo, Larry Shinagawa, Betty Lee Sung, and Christopher Tran, for providing valuable feedback. Thanks to Anne Brown and Paul Hibbard for their technical support. My sincere appreciation to mom, dad and Ken, for giving me a story to write and my love and thanks to my children, Jennifer, Brian, David, and son-in-law Sean, for understanding why this book had to be written. And last, but certainly not least, to my grandson Trent, for the comfort in knowing that this story will continue to be shared.

# FROM IRONING BOARD
# TO CORPORATE BOARD

# PROLOGUE

*It was a typical warm and humid June day in Montgomery County, Maryland. The air was thick and heavy as hundreds of people gathered for the Vietnamese Mutual Association's Annual Citizenship Installation at which I was the keynote speaker. As I uttered the words "congratulations" and "welcome" to the hundreds of soon-to-be new citizens who had come to Einstein High School with their families to participate in the special Induction Ceremony, I watched with delight as their faces beamed with pride and filled with the hope of a promising future in their newly adopted country. Suddenly, a deep and powerful range of emotions rushed through me as I recalled my own family's immigrant journey more than 50 years before.*

*Mama, Ken and Ginny arriving at New York's Idyllwild*
*Airport on March 14, 1954*

# 1

## Meeting Baba in America

"You are going to meet your father," Mama said. Although I was six years old, and my brother Yut-Kew five, we sensed immediately that our lives were going to change. I had not seen my father since I was one year old, too young an age to even hold a recollection of the man I called Baba. Yut-Kew had never met him.

When Mama broke the news, we were already on the airplane. Yut-Kew and I were thrilled to be traveling by airplane to a faraway place. I had only been on an airplane once, when my family left China in 1950 because the communist Chinese government had taken control of the country. I was two years old. We left Ng Nor Hoe Toon, a village in Canton, China, where I was born, for Hong Kong. Ng Nor Hoe Toon was Baba's family village and home to the Ng clan. Mama was a Moy from Moy Nor Lock Toon. As was the custom, after Mama married Baba, she left her village and moved in to live with Baba's family.

*Ginny, age 2*

*Ken, almost 2*

*Mama, Ken (age 2), and Ginny (age 3)*

We had lived for four years with Baba's family in Hong Kong. Then one day seemingly without warning, Mama packed our bags, dressed us in our finest clothes and bundled us into new coats. As we were saying goodbye to relatives at the airport, I had no idea that we were leaving Hong Kong forever and moving to America. I thought we were going on vacation.

The trip to America was difficult for the three of us. Mama suffered miserably from motion sickness and vomited almost the entire time she was awake. Thank goodness the little white air sickness bags were

*Mama, 1950s*

always within reach in the seat pockets in front of us. We felt bad that Mama wasn't feeling well and were relieved whenever she slept, which was most of

the time. As the big sister, I had to take care of Yut-Kew and make sure he was good and kept quiet. Mama had stuffed our Northwest Airlines carry-on bags with snacks of dried gizzards, salted and sweet preserved plums purchased before the flight left. She knew the plums were our favorites, and bought them as a special reward to keep us out of trouble. For those endless hours all we did was eat, sleep and talk to each other as Mama didn't allow us to talk to anyone else on the plane.

On March 14, 1954, after a long and grueling three-day trip by plane, with stops in Japan and Seattle, we finally arrived at New York's Idyllwild Air-

*Baba, 1950s*

port. We represented the newest wave of Chinese immigrants in a 100-year migration history from China to the United States. By setting foot at the airport, we caused a slight bump in the 150,005 Chinese American population, a mere fraction of the total U.S. population at the time.

From the late 1800s to the early 1900s, many laws were passed by Congress to keep the Chinese from immigrating to America, from owning land or businesses, and from marrying anyone. When the mammoth earthquake in 1906 struck San Francisco, all the immigration and birth records in California were destroyed and government officials could not verify who was or was not a U.S. citizen. Because this created a loophole, many Chinese in the U.S. were able to claim they were American citizens. Since children of U.S. citizens were still being permitted entry into the U.S. at that time, many Chinese were able to claim children they still had back in China. As the immigration laws became more restrictive, some Chinese began to claim more children than they actually had, while others would claim children they never had at all. Many of the Chinese American citizens returned to China to bring children to America, some claimed children they didn't really have by selling their last name to anyone looking to immigrate to America. These children came to be known as "paper sons."

Baba was one of the thousands who seized the chance to come to America as a paper son and took the paper name of Eng Duck Sun as his name. Baba was only 20 years old when he began his journey in 1937 to America through Vancouver, in western Canada. From there, he took a train to Montreal and boarded a ship bound for New York. But before he could step foot onto U.S. soil, he had to go through Ellis Island for interrogation by immigration officials.

Ellis Island was quite a harrowing experience for Baba – one that he would never forget. He was placed in a "holding room," which felt like a prison, for about 3 weeks along with many other immigrants until it was his turn to be questioned. When the time for his interview came, he was very nervous because he knew if he did not answer the questions correctly, he could be sent back to China. He studied hard, reviewing all the letters exchanged between him and his "paper father." The immigration officials asked such questions as "How many brothers and sisters do you have?" and "Describe your home in the village?" Thankfully, the time spent on studying the letters paid off and after answering all the questions correctly, Baba was permitted entry into the United States.

Baba's first job in America was as a waiter in a Chinatown restaurant in New York City. He worked very hard day after day and sent money back home to his family in China. This was very typical of many Chinese men living in America. The men who came to America without their families were part of the "bachelor societies" located in America's Chinatowns. Their daily lives consisted of working and playing mahjong in the streets, the back rooms of stores and restaurants, and the family associations. Originated in China, mahjong is a game similar to gin-rummy but played with ivory tiles on which Chinese characters are painted.

Baba belonged to the Eng Family Association. Each surname had its own *gung sor*, or association, such as the Lee Association, Chin Association, or Wong Association. Along with the Eng Association, these were some of the largest associations in Chinatown. Baba went to the Eng Association as often as possible. When I grew up, Baba shared many stories with me about the association members and what villages they came from in China. If we happened to meet an association member, Baba would say, "Fay-Jin, say hello to your Aunt (or Uncle)."

In 1943, Baba was drafted into the U.S. Army during World War II. As a PFC (Private First Class) Baba was stationed in Watertown, New York, and sent to school part time where he, and many others, were taught English. After about a year, he was promoted to a T4 Sergeant 1st Cook. The rank insignia for the U.S. Army was modified in 1942 during World War II to add the rank of Technician for those who had spe-

*Baba in his U.S. Army uniform, 1943*

cial skills or duties such as cooks or mechanics. A T5 was a "corporal," while T4 and T3s were "sergeants." Technicians had no command authority and could not issue orders. In 1946, Baba was sent overseas to Manila in the Philippines and later he participated in the occupation of Japan.

Baba was proud to serve his country during World War II. Although he was not a real "sergeant," he was "First Chef" responsible for feeding thousands of troops. After the war, all veterans were eligible under the GI bill for assistance with education expenses, home and business loans, job search assistance and unemployment pay. Had he not been a citizen, he would have been eligible for permanent residency or citizenship under another law called the Second War Powers Act. The law was passed in 1942 to naturalize soldiers who were not citizens when they enlisted or were drafted. The law was an important symbol to immigrants who had made sacrifices for their adopted country.

Some of Baba's favorite memories while serving in the Army were of his culinary skills. He was an "expert" with making corned beef and mashed potatoes and would always tell us how he prepared the two dishes in the army – with such pride. "People love it," he would say. "Gotta check the time…not cook too much, not cook too little." To this day, Baba continues to tell these stories and remains an active leader with the Kimlau Chinese Memorial American Legion Post 1291 in New York's Chinatown.

After years of living thousands of miles apart, we were finally here waiting to be united as a family. Baba had left China in 1936, shortly after marrying Mama, to find work overseas. He returned in May of 1947, only to leave again in early December of 1948. He was in China to witness my birth, but had to return to America before the birth of Yut-Kew in early September of 1949. Today, Baba was at the airport to

*Baba the chef*

meet his son, Yut-Kew, for the first time. *After all these years, how would he know what we looked like? Would he recognize us? And what about Mama? How would she feel about seeing her husband whom she had married when she was only 17 and he was 19?*

15

Mama and Baba had an arranged marriage; their
fate rested in the hands of their parents. It was be-

*Mama, Baba and Ginny, 1948*

lieved that parents knew what was best for their children and selected mates that would meet specific criteria. Mama's parents were convinced that Baba, coming from the same region in China (Taishan), would be a good provider. That was always a priority consideration. As is tradition in the Chinese culture, my parents met for the first time on their wedding day. *Would they feel like strangers after being apart for most of their 18 years of marriage?* Many questions raced through our heads as we stood waiting patiently for the man who would take us to our new home.

Since I was only one when Baba left China, I had very little memory of him, only what others told me. Mama told us that Baba sent money home regularly for us to live on. We lived with our relatives in Hong Kong in a crowded house with curtains that were hung and stretched from wall to wall creating additional walls for makeshift sleeping areas. We kept a picture

of Baba on a little table along with other family pictures in the family room. Mama would often point

*Farewell at Hong Kong Airport with Ai-Yee, 1954*

out the picture of Baba to us, reminding us how far away he was and how hard he was working to care for us. I wondered, *What is Baba like? Was he nice or was he mean? He didn't look mean, but looked very stern.*

The airport in America was a strange place with people communicating in words we couldn't understand. People had different colored hair and different looking eyes. *Their eyes were so big and round! Why were they staring at us? We must look very different to them too.* People seemed to be in such a hurry. *Where were they rushing off to? And so many of them!* I clutched Mama's hand as tight as I could, feeling scared. Mama held our hands even tighter and warned, "Fay-Jin, Yut-Kew, stay close to me and don't wander away." I knew that Mama was apprehensive but did not want to show it.

# 2

# A Family Reunited

s we glanced around into the crowd, I saw a man whose face looked familiar. I recognized him from the picture on the table at home in Hong Kong. It was Baba and he was walking toward us. It was strange, and yet exciting. I knew this man, and yet I didn't.

He greeted Mama in the typical Chinese fashion, very serious, formal, cordial, and somewhat awkward. But it was obvious that he was glad to see us. He shook my hand firmly as if to say "welcome." It was a warm feeling to hear my father call me, Fay-Jin. "How was your trip? Have you eaten yet?" he politely asked. He then took me by the hand and led us out of the airport. Our life as new immigrants in America began that day in New York City, at Idyllwild Airport, now called Kennedy Airport.

Baba had found an apartment for us to live in the heart of New York City, in an area called Times Square, on 42nd Street, between Eighth and Ninth Avenues. *What a strange place. People and lights everywhere. So many cars! So much noise!* Mama always grabbed our hands and kept us close to her while crossing the busy streets. There were people sleeping on the sidewalks and in front of doorways. Frightened, I asked her, "Why is that man sleeping on the street?" "In America, some people don't have money or jobs, so this is what happens to them," Baba replied.

We stopped in front of a dingy looking building. Baba entered and we stayed close behind him. We walked up a narrow, creaky, dusty, smelly flight of stairs to the second floor. We turned right and stopped at the second doorway where he opened the door. As we walked in, the first thing I saw was the living room. After entering through the front door, I saw two bedrooms, one bathroom and a kitchen with a large metal table. Mama looked around knowing this would be our home now. It was different from what she had imagined. I could see she was worried about living in a neighborhood that appeared to be unsafe.

Mama immediately took over and began organizing things in our new home. The first order of business was to put away our belongings, which didn't take long since we had so little. "This is your room, Fay-Jin," Mama told me. "You and Yut-Kew will be sharing the room." Mama handing out orders was a sign of how things were going to be. She became the strong wife and mother who made sure that everything went well at home. This was natural for her since she had functioned in the role of a single parent all the years in China.

In China, there was plenty of open space for children to run and play. In Hong Kong we didn't have as much open space. However, even though the streets were busy, we were able to play with nearby friends and not worry so much about safety. Here in New York City, Mama would not let us leave the apartment and go outside to play by ourselves. Safety was an issue, so the apartment and our bedroom became our world. There was a window in the room I shared with Yut-Kew that looked out onto the street. *So many lights. So many people!* The only time we were allowed to leave the apartment was to go with Mama to buy food. Sometimes we would take the subway to Chinatown, but Mama didn't like shopping in Chinatown a lot. She always preferred to stay home and be with family, not socializing with others as Baba did.

Baba's cousin and his wife were the first relatives we met in America. We called Baba's cousin "Sek-Ging Gau," which means Uncle Sek-Ging and his wife "Oy-Fong Thoe," which means Aunt Oy-Fong. Uncle Sek-Ging was very thin and reminded me of pictures I had seen of the singer Frank Sinatra. He was very nice and spoke perfect English. Aunt Oy-Fong was very chatty and bilingual, speaking both perfect English and Chinese. She was a little taller than Uncle Sek-Ging and very westernized in the way she dressed.

As our English improved, we began calling Uncle Sek-Ging and Aunt Oy-Fong by their English names, Uncle Bob and Aunt Jenny. "Your children should have English names," Aunt Jenny told Mama and Baba. "It would make it much easier for them to be accepted and make friends at school." "We wouldn't trust anyone else but you to give our children their English names," my parents said to Aunt Jenny. So,

*Aunt Jenny's family and our family, 1958*

Aunt Jenny gave me the name Ginny, taken from my Chinese name Fay-Jin and gave my brother the name Ken, taken from his Chinese name Yut-Kew.

Aunt Jenny was our connection to the new world. Uncle Bob owned a restaurant and knew everyone in

Chinatown. They had two children, Kathy and Carol, who were a couple of years younger than Ken and me. Mama and Baba could not afford, nor did they have the means, to take us anywhere special. Ken and I went on many family outings with Uncle Bob and Aunt Jenny, Kathy and Carol. They took us everywhere in their car. Uncle Bob and Aunt Jenny taught us strategies for survival in America and were always willing to answer our questions about being "American." They were always there whenever I needed someone to speak with my parents about issues I was dealing with. Mama and Baba had a very difficult time understanding what I was going through and were often very stubborn, but Uncle Bob and Aunt Jenny were able to explain that things were done differently in America. In most cases, situations improved afterward.

Baba was a waiter at the Rathskeller Chinese restaurant located in a basement on Mott Street in the
heart of Chinatown. He was proud of his job as a
waiter and knew everything about each and every
Chinese restaurant in Chinatown. He considered him-
self a connoisseur of Chinese food and loved to visit
other Chinese restaurants to compare menus and
prices. Every time Baba passed a Chinese restaurant,
Ken and I had to go in with him and wait while he
chatted with the owners and waiters. Sometimes the
owners would give us scoops of ice cream, which we
enjoyed, but in most cases Ken and I were very bored.

Baba sometimes cooked for us at home. One of
his favorite dishes was won ton soup – which was the
best! He and I made won tons together making a game
of who would make them faster. As we made the won
tons, Baba told me stories about how he learned to
make them while working in a restaurant. He was very

impressed that I was able to wrap the tiny dumplings at a fast speed. Baba chuckled – which was something he would do whenever he was impressed, in agreement, or was proud of what Mama, Ken or I did or said.

Baba also made the best mouth-watering stew with tender chunks of lamb, *foo jook* (bean curd sticks), mushrooms and lots of Chinese spices and flavorings. One of the ingredients that gave the stew the distinctive taste was the fermented bean curd that came in a glass jar and seemed to last forever in the refrigerator. I loved the smell of the stew simmering for hours over the stovetop. Eating and going to Chinatown were Baba's favorite pastimes. At every meal, Baba expected soup and plenty of rice. To accommodate his wishes, we always had a big pot of soup simmering on the stove with a smell that permeated the house and was always inviting.

Mama was the one who made sure we all stayed healthy and strong. She was an expert in making delicious soups with ingredients such as chicken, black mushrooms, winter melon, tofu, and Chinese herbs. She was a great believer in traditional Chinese herbal medicine and made soups containing ingredients such as lotus seeds, ginseng, roots, dates, red beans, etc. If any of us was sick or not feeling well, Mama would boil Chinese herbs and make us drink an entire bowl. Later, whenever I came home from college and did not look "healthy" according to Mama, I would be forced to drink several bowls of medicinal soup. Since she made the soups with chicken broth and they generally tasted pretty good, I actually didn't mind drinking them.

But there were some soups made from herbs that were not very tasty. We always knew when those soups were cooking because the entire house would smell.

*Ewww! It looked and smelled yucky!* I always had to hold my nose when drinking those nasty medicinal-tasting soups – but I did end up drinking whatever was made for me. I didn't have the heart to hurt Mama's feelings.

Cow's brain was known to have the capability to cure headaches and if anyone of us complained about having headaches, Mama would ask Baba to bring back a package of cow's brain from the Chinese supermarket in Chinatown. This was added to fresh chicken and simmered over low heat for hours. Once we knew what went into the soup, we rarely complained of headaches.

One thing Mama always talked about was the importance of "yin and yang," which keeps the body balanced with what she called "hot foods" and "cold foods." If we were eating too many fried foods, which were considered to be "hot foods," Mama would make sure that we balanced it off with eating foods like watermelon, which she considered a "cold food." It was not unusual for Mama not to eat something because it was *nget hee* (a hot food) for she didn't want to be "off-balance." Perhaps Mama knew best. Over the years, we stayed in good health with no major health problems. In fact, Ken and I were the recipients of perfect attendance records in school for a number of years.

Our new life revolved around work and school. Rarely did my family venture to find new experiences. So I remember being particularly excited one day when I was seven, Baba came home from working at the restaurant with a proposal. "Mama," he said, "We should enter Fay-Jin in the beauty contest in Chinatown for little girls. The winner gets $100!" Mama went through her usual routine of complaining and protesting when anything different was suggested, but after thinking more and more about the $100 prize, she eventually gave in and let me become a contestant in the Little Miss Chinatown Beauty Contest.

It was the summer of 1955 and the beauty pageant was being held in Memorial Park in Chinatown. Aunt Jenny was there to make sure that I dressed appropriately. My bowl-styled haircut was combed to shiny perfection. I had on a beautiful new print dress with pleats that were crisply starched and pressed. I also had on a new pair of black, shiny patent leather Mary-Jane shoes and white socks with tiny delicate lace edging around the cuff. "Remember to smile at the judges," Aunt Jenny advised me. She had told me all I had to do was walk up and down the runway, and smile. It sounded pretty easy. To Mama and Baba's surprise, I won one of the two first prizes because, as

Baba explained that I was "fair skinned, plump, and had a nice smile."

Life in New York City became a disappointment for my parents, particularly Mama. She did not want to raise her children in an environment where people slept in front of our doorway and on nearby streets. She had traveled too far and wanted a better life for her family. "Our children cannot grow up like this," she said to Baba. "We need to have a business and work hard so that Fay-Jin and Yut-Kew can have a good life." And so, Mama and Baba began saving their money to buy a business. Another chapter in our lives as Americans was about to begin.

# 3

# Opening the Chinese Hand Laundry

In 1957, we learned that the owner of a Chinese laundry in Long Island, New York, was selling his business for $1,500. Mama and Baba seriously discussed the idea of buying the business and moving to Long Island. Several of my parent's friends already had thriving laundry businesses, but $1,500 was a lot of money at the time for us. Finally, Mama and Baba decided that going into the laundry business would be good for the family. Luckily, they were able to borrow the money from two of their cousins. Amazingly, through hard work and long hours, they managed to pay back the loan in one year.

The laundry business was ideal for Mama and Baba because they need not be fluent in English to

*Ginny, 1958*

run the business successfully. While Baba knew enough English to communicate with the customers, Mama knew very little.

Our new home on Long Island was on Hillside Avenue in Williston Park. For the next 31 years, this would be Mama and Baba's place of business as well as their home. In looking back I can only imagine what a proud moment it was for both of them be-cause in America owning your own business was a sure sign of success.

When we ar-rived at our new home, Ken and I

*Ginny by the front door, 1960*

ran around excitedly. I thought proudly, "The whole

37

building belongs to us. It's like a palace." We would not have to worry about people living above or below us, and most wonderful of all, sleeping in front of our doorway. Mama and Baba definitely could not complain about the commute from home to work and back. They simply had to leave the front half of the building space where they operated the laundry, and go to other side of the curtain to reach our residence in the back half of the space. Only a curtain that stretched from one end of the opening to the other separated the two worlds. "This reminds me of the wall of curtains in our old home back in Hong Kong," Mama said.

I wanted our new home to have a nice appearance. We did not have doors. We only had curtains. When the curtains were drawn, we felt we had as much privacy as if actual doors existed. In addition to having curtains that separated the store from our living quarters, we hung drapes to separate each room. I hated the drapes. They were cheap and mismatched hand-me-downs. After several years, I finally purchased blue and white upholstery fabric from a store near Chinatown off of Delancey Street. Since Baba did not want to spend money on purchasing a sewing machine, I took on the tedious task of sewing them by hand. It took me almost a week to complete the sewing, but when they were finished and hung, I felt a great sense of accomplishment.

Our home was sparsely furnished. The only real pieces of furniture we owned were our beds, dressers, cast-off wooden chairs from a Chinese restaurant and metal closets that we purchased to store our nicest belongings. Decades later, my parents still have the metal closets in their room.

Over time, our home also became filled with hand-me-downs from customers and friends. *New clothes! New toys!* Ken and I would think excitedly as customers brought bags of used clothing and toys to the store along with their dirty laundry. We loved to rummage through the bags and find new treasures. It felt like Christmas.

Our home was actually equivalent to a two-bedroom apartment. Ken and I shared bedroom space in a very narrow hallway that measured about 9 by 12 feet. We had a bunk bed, a chair, and a used small dresser. Passing through our "bedroom" to the left was the small living room, where we watched television. Mama and Baba's bedroom was located behind the living room. To ventilate the house, especially in the summer months, we propped open a door accessible from the living room that led to the back yard.

Our home was always dimly lit. *Why aren't the light bulbs more powerful?* I wondered. Whenever Ken and I came home from school, we would turn all the lights

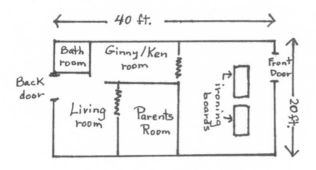

*Drawing of the back of laundry*

on in the house. As soon as we left a space, Mama came and turned off the lights. "Conserve electricity. Don't waste money," Mama would admonish us.

I wanted our home to look like the homes of my friends who lived in big fancy houses on the other side of the railroad tracks. Downstairs, we had a basement with concrete floor and walls that was dominated by a large old oil tank in the back. To access the basement, we could walk down through a lift-up door from the floor of the laundry or from the outside through a slanted metal pull-up double door like in *The Wizard of Oz.*

One day I asked Mama, "Can I please decorate the basement?" She frowned. "Why do you want to waste time and money? It is fine the way it is," she asked. But I was hopeful. I knew from her tone that as long as I did not ask her for money and used my allowance money, she would not object. In Mama's view, the family budget was earmarked for basic essentials such as food and housing only. Home improvement was a frivolous luxury.

I quickly set to work. I painted the entire basement's concrete floor with maroon paint. I covered the old sofa that the former tenants left behind with a piece of extra fabric I found around the house. And then I finished the room with a new plastic tablecloth over the kitchen table.

As a result, our living quarters increased in size. We used the basement as our kitchen and dining room. Eventually, it also doubled as a family den. When we entertained guests, we gathered in the basement where we would sit on the hard chairs and the old sofa. Mama always prepared plenty of home cooked meals for our friends. "Eat, you eat more," she urged. No one ever left our home hungry.

Years later, we indulged in a luxury accessory for the basement – a bathtub, along with a half wall erected for privacy. In the past, we took baths in a very large basin. To prepare a bath, we had to lug large buckets of water to fill the basin, and empty out the water in those same buckets afterward. It was a laborious chore. How wonderful it was to be able to turn the water faucet on and take a bath in a tub! We did not take modern conveniences for granted.

The house was feeling like a real home. Although we didn't have a white picket fence, we found a way to create our own garden. Across a commercial parking lot outside behind the laundry, there was a small patch of dirt no larger than six feet long and two feet wide. If anyone knew how to make a plant grow anywhere, it was Mama. All Mama had to do was stick a stem down into the dirt and before you knew it, plants would grow. Soon, she had *gow-gee*, a Chinese herb that the Chinese believe contains nutrients for improving one's eyesight, growing everywhere. Mama made chicken soup with the leaves and added liver, making sure that the liver was cooked just right – not too well done. It was so delicious! I didn't care that it was good for me; I just loved the taste. Ken, on the other hand, compared it with having to take awful medicine. He hated it.

*Poor Ken.* He also could not stomach some other Chinese delicacies. On special occasions, Mama made *yuen*, a special soup in which balls of sticky dough

*Yuen, the sticking dough soup*

were dropped in along with scallions, Chinese radishes, and other vegetables. I could easily have eaten 2 or 3 bowls in one sitting but Ken hated those globs of dough and had difficulty swallowing them without choking. Baba insisted that Ken remain seated at the table until he finished the whole bowl. I always felt sorry for him. Ken would sit and sit until no one was around and then press the sticky *yuen* against the underside of the table. I knew what Ken had done but kept his secret. Baba would return and say, "Now wasn't that delicious?"

As Ken and I thoroughly explored our new neighborhood, we found that we really liked it. Our laundry was situated in the middle of a block along with several other businesses. To the left was Mr. Sidney Wechter, owner of an appliance store, and to the extreme end of the block was Mr. Mahoney, owner of Mahoney's Restaurant. To the right was Mrs. Billingsley, manager of a candy store where we would occasionally purchase our snacks. Next to the candy store was Maria of Maria's Leather Repair Shop.

I always looked forward to running errands for Mama and Baba because it gave me a chance to walk down the block and stop in at the stores to chat with the owners. Mama never understood why I, a young girl, would want to socialize with people I hardly knew.

When I finally returned home after the errands, Mama would say, "Fay-Jin, where you go? To China to buy milk? Good Chinese girls don't talk so much. Such a waste of time, talking to everybody. If you have time, you should be studying or come and help at the store." I wanted to blurt in response, "Well then, I don't want to be a good Chinese girl." But I knew better than to provoke Mama into another endless lecture. My opportunity to explore the world outside the laundry would come in due time.

*Sign of the Chinese Hand Laundry*

Meanwhile, the laundry was our home base. At the start of the business day, we drew the window curtains open from the inside of the glass panels that comprised the whole front side of the laundry. From the outside, the drawn curtains revealed the sign "Chinese Hand Laundry." At dusk, we turned on the neon lights of the sign. At closing time, we turned off the sign and closed the curtains.

The laundry was open for business every day for more than 30 years. The laundry business was our livelihood, our platform in American society and our home of cherished memories. When we opened the Chinese Hand Laundry, we began a new chapter in our lives as Chinese Americans.

# 4

# Life Behind the Ironing Board

*Ginny and Ken in front of the store, 1962*

A customer who walked in through the front door of the laundry would head straight for the counter to place their loads of dirty laundry. Behind the counter was the heart of the laundry – two ironing boards. On the sides, shelves lined the walls. The shelves stored neatly arranged packages of freshly laundered clothing. And on the floor were a few wooden stools.

The two ironing boards were the focal points around which our business and family activities revolved. Mama and Baba spent hours working behind the two ironing boards almost every single day of the year for more than 30 years. They worked side by side, facing the front window that looked out onto the street while conversing with each other in Chinese.

They usually conversed about what to cook for the next meal and the progress Ken and I were making at school and other family matters. Actually, they weren't exchanging dialogues so much as Mama would talk most of the time, and Baba would simply nod or speak briefly. Sometimes Baba initiated conversations related to Chinatown or what was happening with members of the Eng Association or the Kimlau Post.

Not unlike many Chinese families, we did not have open family discussions. The parents talked while the children listened or talked to each other. There was no cross-generational conversation at the dinner table like with our friends' families. We never shared our feelings. Families communicated through silence, impregnated with high expectations and cultural mores. As time wore on, however, the lack of communication became less culturally-driven as Ken and I gradually lost our ability to speak our parents' native tongue.

At the laundry, I would recognize from the smell of the distinct odor of melting wax that Mama and

Baba were trying to smooth the scratches from the bottom of their irons. They would run the irons back and forth over a thin layer of wax placed on squares of damask cloth. They were always very careful to make sure that the wax was completely melted before placing the iron back onto a customer's item of clothing.

While other kids did homework on desks or on their kitchen tables, we did ours on the ironing board. Since the ironing boards were the only flat surfaces available to us, they became our makeshift desks on which homework assignments were completed. Ken would use one of the ironing boards and I would use the other. Mama expected us to cover the surface with a large piece of cardboard to keep it clean and free of ink marks. Of course, the ironing boards were only available to us when Mama and Baba were not using them, or late in the evening and on weekends.

*Mama at the ironing board, 1966*

We also turned the ironing boards into our play areas. Underneath the ironing boards was a large open space. Usually the space was taken up by customers' individual collections of clothes that were tied together by the shirt sleeves or bundled inside pillow cases. The clothes sometimes smelled of human sweat. But after the clothes were sent off to be pressed, Ken and

53

I claimed the open space as our private play area to hide-and-seek and to play house.

We did not have toys to play with, forcing Ken and me to be very creative in what we did for fun. One of my favorite games was playing "school." We would take out our school books and pretended class was in session. One of Mama's friends gave us a small blackboard as a gift – which was a cherished item and as important as books in our pretend classroom. Of course, I was always the teacher and Ken was always the student. Sometimes we would envision a library in the corner of the laundry and pretend to lend books to each other, issue fines for overdue books, and advise each other on how to locate a particular book in the library. And just like a real library, we used index cards to record the due dates and glued envelopes to old books to hold the cards. Although a child's play, I aspired to teach in a real classroom.

We also passed the time playing our favorite board game, Candyland. We played for hours on end when

*Mama and Baba by the front counter, 1968*

our neighbor Carol, who lived above the candy store next door, brought her game over. Sometimes when it was too hot to be indoors, we played outside on a table placed on the sidewalk in front of the laundry.

During the winter holidays, we'd decorate the laundry counter with a miniature artificial Christmas tree adorned with 10 or so tiny Christmas ornaments. Ken and I would wrap boxes, sometimes empty, and put them under the tree to make it look as though we would be receiving a lot of presents. One Christmas I saved enough money to purchase a phonograph record player for Ken. I wrapped it up beautifully and proudly tried to place it under the Christmas tree, but the box was so large it wouldn't fit on the narrow counter. I had to place it on the ironing board closest to the tree instead. "It is the best gift I've ever received," Ken told me.

Like every Chinese laundry, we also had a number of wooden stools. One of Mama's many hidden talents was building stools with only a slab of wood nailed to shorter pieces on the two ends. A wooden stool was a necessity because much of the work in laundries was done close to the floor, such as sorting, labeling and packaging. Over the years, I spent a lot

of time sitting on those stools and even ate many meals
on them as well.

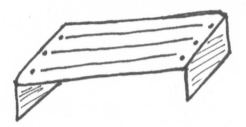

*Drawing of the sitting stool*

The seasons came and went, but there was one
major challenge to the summer season at the laundry.
Chinese laundries were sooooooo hot! The fans were
on all day and night during the summer months since
there was no air conditioning. We even used cardboard
cut from old cereal boxes or pieces of paper folded in
accordion style as hand fans. Since our building was
one long continuous space, we would prop open the
doors in both the front of the store and the back of

the house to create a refreshing draft. Mama used to say, "See, we don't need air conditioning."

During the winter months, the nature of our business kept us warmer than most buildings. In the laundry, we had the heat from the irons constantly in use and the steam generated from cooking the starch for the shirts. In our small residence, we were kept warm from the heated stove, always simmering with pots of Mama's dishes and delicious soup. Between our business practices and Mama's diligence in turning off lights, we managed to keep electricity costs to a minimum. However, since the laundry was not very well insulated, we had to diligently seal the gaps between the doors and floors/walls with rags and cloths.

Week by week, we followed the same multi-step cleaning process that took approximately five days to complete. Saturday was always our busiest day of the week. On Saturday, we would sort and mark clothes received on Friday and Saturday.

On Monday mornings, a contracted cleaning company picked up the bundled and labeled dirty clothes and returned them washed the next day. That afternoon, we would sort the cleaned clothes and apply starch or other specially requested treatments.

We made the starch ourselves, and controlled the thickness to accommodate the customers who had requested varying degrees of starch on their collars. I usually helped by mixing the starch powder with boiling water to get a translucent consistency, like liquid glue but with a thicker consistency. The powdery, chalky smell of the heated starch permeated the laundry. After the starch cooled to the point where we would not burn our hands, Mama and I would take a clean shirt, bunch up the collar along with the top half of the button and buttonhole sections, dip it into the mixture and squeeze out the excess. We started with the shirts that had to be treated with heavy starch and then diluted the mixture for regular starch and diluted it further for light starch. After the shirts were starched, they were ready for pickup by another contracted company for pressing. Customers who had their shirts regularly pressed paid twenty cents per shirt in the early years. Customers who wanted their shirts "hand-ironed" paid an extra five cents. For this custom service, instead of sending them out, Mama and Baba would keep the shirts in the laundry and manually pressed them.

On Thursdays, we received the pressed shirts back from the contracted company. My parents immediately began sorting and packaging them in brown wrapping paper which came in large, heavy rolls. The rolls were so heavy we had to help Baba put them in the holder, which had a very sharp built-in cutting blade for cutting the paper to size. The shirts and bed sheets were folded in a special manner so that each finished package was tied with a white string and measured approximately 10 inches wide and 14 inches long. That way, all the packages would fit on the shelves in nice, neatly stacked rows. As a final step, we would place the laundry ticket on the front of the package where it would be easily seen.

Most customers came on a weekly basis to pick up and drop off. On occasions, customers would forget to pick up their items and leave them with us for years.

Although Mama knew very little English, she managed her own way of communication with customers. To track a customers' laundry, she created her own unique code system. She knew the letters of the alphabet and numbers. Whenever a new customer came into the laundry, Mama used a permanent marker and arbitrarily marked the inside of shirt collars with a series of letters and numbers on new items of clothing to be cleaned. Mama was not able to read or write in English; the letters and numbers were randomly selected. However, when it was my turn to create a laundry mark for a new customer, I took liberties and used letters that formulated words. The next time the same customer returned, we would continue to use

*Shirt collar with laundry markings*

the same combination of letters and numbers on new items. Since Mama never needed to know customers' names, she always identified her customers by the codes she had created on their laundry labels. Although

Mama relied on matching the numbers on tickets that were given to customers when the laundry was dropped off, she had a list of regular customers and their special codes memorized in her head. Whenever she saw the customers approaching the laundry, she would have their packages out before they took out their tickets.

We remembered "MART" as one of our most regular customers. He came into the laundry with five to six shirts each week for years. Then there was "MIT," another regular customer. He lived in Garden City and always asked for heavy starch, the heavier the better. He liked the collars of his shirts to be very stiff and crisp. Mama always dipped his shirts into the starch mixture first before diluting the mixture for other customers. We knew "SCHVI" as the customer who would bring large loads of sheets, pillow cases, shirts and other items every two weeks, all stuffed into one pillow case.

One day, when Mama and I spotted customer "8HR" and his wife at the supermarket, Mama pointed to them and said to me, "Look, Fay-Jin, there's 8HR." I knew exactly who she was talking about. I had many conversations with this customer but never knew his real name.

Even though Mama may not have known her customers' names, she maintained a good rapport with them. On occasions, she gave plant cuttings as gifts for her most loyal customers. Mama nurtured a plant garden alongside the store's glass window front, where the plants flourished under the southern exposure to the sun. Mama's pride and joy was the jade plant that grew very full – more than 3 feet wide. She would modestly accept the customers' compliments of her garden.

When Mama did try to converse in English, I was a little fearful what she would actually say. Mama always admired people who were plump, a sign to her that they were healthy. Once, I overheard Mama tell a customer, "You lucky, you fat." I was mortified. But it was too late. All I could do was apologize to the customer explaining that Mama was actually giving her a compliment. "Mama! Do not tell American people they are fat. It's insulting," I told her. But Mama did not understand.

While it seemed we never left the laundry, all of us except Mama had individual life experiences outside of the laundry. Ken and I attended school and made friends. Baba took outside jobs on occasions and socialized in Chinatown. However, Mama was a different story. She never left the laundry, focusing only on serving her daily customers. Mama had always been the same way even prior to coming to the

United States. In China and in Hong Kong, she was always busy working and had neither time nor interest in socializing. She primarily focused on caring for the family. To her, any other matter was a distraction of time and energy. Among Mama's rare indulgences, however, was television. Mama loved the Ed Sullivan, Lucille Ball and wrestling shows.

To Mama's dismay, Baba socialized a lot in Chinatown. Mama couldn't understand why Baba loved to go to Chinatown since she herself did not enjoy socializing there. My parents' number one contentious argument revolved around gambling. They argued heatedly for several years over Baba's gambling, even though Baba gambled only occasionally and did not gamble for high stakes money. Mama always left the discussions in tears. She felt that any gambling was an unforgivable waste of money and precious time.

Even though I did not gamble, Mama would draw parallels between Baba and me. "Aiya, Fay-Jin," Mama would say. At that point, I braced myself since Chinese people say "aiya" when they wanted to express surprise or frustration. "You and your father are just alike….always going out and socializing – What a waste of time!"

Overall as a family, we rarely socialized. During the weekdays, visitors rarely dropped by since the majority of our friends also were busy working in Chinese laundries. We only had free time after business hours or on weekends. Since we did not own a car, and no one was licensed to drive, we were never able to visit friends unless they lived within walking distance. The laundry business exacted high commitment and sacrifice from our entire family, often at the expense of work/life balance, but our economic station and Mama's work ethic also tethered us closely to the laundry.

# 5

# New School,
# New Lessons

In May 1957, Baba, the only one in the family who knew a little English, took Ken and me to register for school while Mama tended the store. We walked two blocks to a large, red brick building. "Cross Street Elementary School" looked like a huge brick fortress. Children were outside playing. *Will I make new friends here?* I wondered. When we walked into the building, some children walking down the hall stared and pointed at us. Others giggled. A few even tried to speak to us but we didn't really understand what they were saying.

School officials placed both Ken and me in the same second grade class since neither of us were able to speak English, even though I was over a year older than my brother. I looked up at Baba, silently pleading, "Baba, don't leave us in this scary place. I feel very strange here. I don't know if I belong." My brother stayed close to me, also feeling apprehensive. But Baba did not heed my entreaties. "Good luck," Baba said as he gave us his typical firm handshake. Then, he walked away and never turned around to look back. At that moment, we knew that we did not have a choice. We had to stay.

The teacher led us into the classroom. "Class, say hello to Ginny and Ken Eng," she said. I was bewildered. All I heard was our English names. *What should I do? What should I say?* I scanned the unfamiliar faces

Mama and Ginny, 1948.

Ginny (almost 2), Mama, and Ken (almost 1), 1950.

Ginny (age 3) and Ken (age 2) in China.

Ken and Ginny in Hong Kong, 1953.

Baba in the U.S. Army, 1943.

Baba in his younger years.

Mama at age 35.

Ginny, Mama, and Ken, 1953.

Farewell in Hong Kong before leaving for America, 1954.

Ginny, 1955.

Ken, Florence, Mama, and Ginny, 1958.

The Eng family, 1958.

The Eng children, 1963.

Ginny at OCA's Corporate Awards Dinner, 1994.

Ginny with U.S. Postal Service, unveiling the collection series, Honolulu, 2005.

Ginny at Martin Luther King 30 year anniversary march, 1993.

County Executive Doug Duncan (Montgomery, Maryland) Acknowledgement, 2006.

Ginny with Jesse Jackson and Janet Murguia (NCLR), 2006.

Ginny with Secretary of Transportation Norm Mineta, 2007.

Ginny with Congressman Mike Honda, 2007.

Ginny at OCA National Convention, Las Vegas, 2005.

Mama, Baba, Ginny, and Ken, 2004.

Ginny and "Grand Dog" Toni, Christmas, 2004.

David, Brian, Ginny, and Jennifer, Thanksgiving, 2001.

Jenn, Baby Trent, and Sean, December 2007.

in the room. In the back, I caught a glimpse of a girl smiling. I thought, "Someone is smiling at me. She looks like a nice person." Later, the girl, Linda, came over to me and took my hand and spoke. I didn't know what she was saying, but I didn't feel so alone anymore. Linda became one of my closest friends. I discovered she lived within walking distance from our laundry. We played together almost every day after school for years throughout elementary school.

Ken and I had to learn English, as well as adapt to a new school, on our own. The school did not offer classes for students who were learning English as a second language. We did not know any other students who were in our similar situation. My parents were unable to help us since they were limited in English proficiency. Mama knew a few laundry terms: "sheets," which she pronounced "sh*t"; "pillow cases," which were "pooloe case"; and, "shirts" which were "sut." She struggled with pronouncing the letters "r" and "sh" because the sounds did not exist in the Chinese language, just as Americans are unfamiliar with certain foreign sounds in other languages. Since Baba was in America much longer, he had less difficulty with pronouncing phonetic English sounds but he still could not teach us. Our relatives Aunt Jenny and Uncle Bob no longer lived near us and therefore could not lend assistance.

Ken and I did not know it at the time, but we helped ourselves by creating our own full immersion language program. To learn English as quickly as we could, we conversed with each other exclusively in English, even at home. To our own surprise, we learned quickly. But in our desire to learn English, we ended up gradually losing much of our ability to speak our native Chinese language – our main connection to our parents, birth country and heritage. Ken and I rarely spoke English in public out of embarrassment that people would overhear us. Despite my rudimentary Chinese language skills and young age, I often was called to serve as interpreters for our parents with customers, school officials and doctors.

While we could downplay speaking Chinese, we could not hide all things Chinese. For our packed school lunch, Mama gave us a thermos of rice and *lop-tcheurng*, or Chinese sausages. We were a little embarrassed over eating our lunch in the cafeteria. While our friends ate sandwiches, we had rice. But by lunchtime, we were hungry so we simply ate the lunch we had. After school, we always looked forward to a second lunch Mama prepared for us at 3:30 p.m. She always had ready bowls of rice, a plate or two of meat and vegetables and occasionally, soup. Dinner was served late in the evening, around 9:30 p.m.

Every week, we students would line up at school to deposit money into our student bank accounts created to save money for college. My parents were very frugal with money. They stressed SAVE, with a capital "S." "Don't spend money unless it is absolutely necessary" was Mama's motto. I think that Baba felt differently, but he would never speak up against Mama's wishes. College savings were among the few expenses that my parents prioritized. They saved up to give Ken and me 50 cents weekly for our college saving. At the end of the year, we had saved $20.

We received mandatory vaccinations at school. Ken and I were not accustomed to doctors, much less shots. We did not have a family doctor. Nor did we ever have regular checkups. "Doctors are for sick people, not healthy people," Mama said. As the day to receive the vaccination approached, Ken and I became increasingly anxious. "What would it feel like?"

*Baba with Ken and Ginny, 1962*

We stayed up all night worried. As a test, I pinched myself several times hard. "Ouch!" I'd yelp.

While waiting in line for his vaccination, Ken bolted out of the school in fear. The principal escorted him back to the school, and designated me,

Ken's older sister, as the carrier of a message to my parents. "Mama, Baba," I said, "The principal says you have to take Yut-Kew to get his vaccination from a doctor. The school will not do it this time."

Mama and Baba were not pleased. Now, they would have to make an appointment with Dr. Sincoff, a doctor we only visited for dire reasons, pay for a taxicab, take time off from work and pay for Ken's vaccination, when he could have gotten a shot for free at school. Mama and Baba were very firm in making sure that Ken understood he was never to repeat that behavior again.

Mama and Baba did not always understand our school activities. Once, our school gave the students a choice of musical instruments to borrow and take home to play. I brought home a violin and Ken decided on a trumpet. We were so proud and happy with our choices.

"Mama, look what the school gave me so that I can learn to play the violin like the other students." I said. "And look at what they gave me," Ken added, holding up his trumpet with great pride. But Mama immediately said, "You must both return the instruments. What if something happens to them? What if they break? They are very expensive and we cannot afford to pay to repair or replace them." To Ken, she added, "The trumpet is bad for your health." Mama worried that the physical exertion of blowing into the trumpet would affect Ken's circulatory system.

Mama used the tone that meant no one, even Baba, could challenge her. We were very disappointed and embarrassed to return the instruments, but we did. *Why can't we learn to play a musical instrument like the other kids?* I lamented silently, and Ken agreed. Ken and I made up excuses and told the teachers we had changed our minds about playing a musical instrument.

Ken and I were routinely caught between two worlds at school. One day, the school principal called me to the office. "Ginny, your records indicate different birth dates each year," he said, "We need to have one date of birth like everyone else."

Our family follows the lunar calendar. Because the calendar is based on the position of the moon, the days in the lunar calendar change from year to year relative to the Gregorian calendar we commonly use today. According to the lunar calendar, my birthday always falls on the 5th day of the second month of each lunar year. To solve the school record problem, I chose March 15 as my official birthday since my birthday fell on that day that year.

As if the day that we celebrated our birthdays were not complicated enough, we also backdated our date of birth one year. Baba always told us that we are really one year older in Chinese years because before one is born, one has already lived more than 9 months in the womb, which was closer to one year. Therefore, I may be 7 years old on my school records, but it would not be uncommon for Baba to regard me as being 8 years old. I remember seeing the obituaries and the person listed according to his Chinese age. Baba would say, "We list the person's Chinese age

*Chinese calendar showing the 5th day of the 2nd month*

because it means the person is another year older, wiser, and deserving of more respect."

Regardless of my age, I was growing up faster than my years in the United States, as I increasingly took on responsibilities to bridge my parents to the outside world.

# 6

# An Eldest Child's Duty

When I started school, I learned to be my own counsel. We were in a newly adopted country, and I was further along with adapting to the language and culture than my parents.

I remember that one of the momentous decisions I had to make came when my third grade teacher told me at the end of the year, "We'd like you to consider skipping to the next grade," since chronologically, I was older than the other students. I probably was doing well academically to warrant this offer to move me up a grade level. I thought to myself, "What should I do? Should I stay with the friends I had made or skip to the fourth grade as the teacher is recommending." My parents would not understand and were in no position to guide me. I mulled over my options. Finally, I told the teacher I would stay in the third grade, but requested that my brother and I not be placed in the same classroom. I knew it was time for both of us to have our own space. I still kept an eye on him. As the "Number One oldest sister," I felt a responsibility for writing absentee excuses and advising Ken. He rarely listened but I considered it my responsibility anyway.

Being the oldest daughter also meant I was responsible for cooking some of the dinners during weekdays and lunches and dinners on weekends. When I was eight, Mama taught me how to make rice, a staple at every meal. I honed my skills as the family chef through practice over the years allowing Mama and Baba to continue their daily laundry chores.

I was always interested in watching Mama make Chinese dumplings and was right there with my measuring cups and spoons. Mama never measured any of her ingredients; she did everything by instinct. I would ask Mama to not put the ingredients into the mixture until I had a chance to measure with my measuring utensils and record for future use. As a result, I was able to create my own recipe book comprised of the family's favorite dishes and pastries.

One of my favorite recipes was dumplings that are often called *ha-gows*. Mama would mix a bag of wheat starch with about 3 soupspoons of tapioca starch. She would pour approximately a quart of boiling water into the mixture and stir with chopsticks. "Keep the mixture covered until it was cool enough to knead," she would remind me. In the interim, we would chop up pork, shrimp, Chinese mushrooms, and water chestnuts and season to taste with salt, pepper and soy sauce. When the hot mixture had cooled off a bit, we kneaded the mixture until it was well blended. Pieces of the dough were rolled into small rounds and ready for pressing flat. Mama used her large cleaver and pressed the small rounds into thin flat rounds. Years later, Mama found a tortilla press that did the job beautifully. These rounds were then molded into cuplike holders, filled with the meat mixture, sealed closed, and then steamed for about 30 minutes till cooked. The *har-gows* were always perfect – soft, somewhat chewy and very tasty!

Every year, in celebration of the 5th day of the 5th month of the lunar calendar, Mama would prepare to *gwor doong* which meant making glutinous rice wrapped in leaves. I was always delegated as her assistant. *Gwor doong* was quite an ordeal and Mama would make 150 or 200 each time to give to friends and family. Approximately one and one-half month before, Mama would prepare salted eggs by soaking dozens of eggs in salt water. The yolks would get salty and hardened. She would also salt pieces of pork and place them in the refrigerator. Bags and bags of bamboo leaves were soaked in our bathtub and cleaned daily for a week. Then we washed pounds and pounds of glutinous rice and salted to taste. Sometimes Mama added red beans or skinned peanuts to the rice mixture. Since Ken and I did not really care for red beans, she made some special order plain rice ones for us. Mama always knew how much seasoning to add by tasting a few grains of salted raw rice to see if it was salty enough. Then we would slice the salted meat and eggs into small pieces. Some years Mama made sweet ones which were dipped into syrup when eaten, but they were not very popular with the family.

*Picture of* doong *(Chinese tamale)*

When it was time to make the *doongs* Mama and I would sit on our stools to be as close to the ground as possible. We would take 2 or 3 leaves first, overlap them halfway, and then fold in half. We would fold the bottom of the grouped leaves to form a cup-like holder in the palm of our hands, placing the seasoned rice, 2 pieces of eggs and 2 pieces of meat inside. Then one or two more leaves were added on top of the grouping and folded closed. The bundled leaf grouping was tied together with string as tightly as possible. The hard part was keeping all the rice inside the leaves when tying. The end pieces of the leaves were then cut off. The final shape was that of a triangular prism.

When all the *doongs* were made – and there were many – Mama would wash the huge tins in preparation for cooking. The tins were aluminum canisters she had collected over the years from Mahoney's restaurant at the end of the block. She would also collect square pieces of wood and used them as covers when cooking *doongs*.

The *doongs* were cooked in our kitchen in the basement and the smell of leaves cooking would permeate the entire house for hours. This was usually done on Sundays when the store was closed so Mama could focus her full attention without interruption from customers. When the cooking was completed, Mama still had more work to do. Cleaning the stove top and the tins (for storage and use the following year) after hours and hours of sticky rice and leaves bubbling over was a challenge. For the family, Mama's hard work was worth it. We had plenty of delicious *doongs* to eat of our choosing. For the next week or so, we would

*The Eng children in the laundry, 1958*

eat *doongs* for almost every lunch and snack, sometimes for dinner as well.

Two years after arriving in the United States, I
became an older sister again. On December 7, 1956,
my sister, Florence, was born. She was the only one
of the three of us to be born in the United States. I

*The Eng family in the laundry, 1958*

was almost nine and Ken was seven. We were happy
– I was especially happy to have a little sister, someone other than my brother, who would play "school"
with me and be the student.

Our happiness was short-lived. One customer,
who was a physician, told me on a number of occasions over the years, "Your sister looks very pale. Your
parents should take her to see a doctor." I told my
mother each time, but she brushed it off, not wishing
to hear any more about it. Mama didn't trust doctors.
She had seen friends go to the doctor when they appeared well, but later become ill. In reality, these friends
likely were already ill when they saw the doctor. Also,
there was the burden of medical expenses. Mama and
Baba had no health insurance. Reluctantly, after numerous urgings, my parents finally took Florence to
see a doctor who diagnosed her with a disease called
Cooley's Anemia. That news had a drastic impact on

my family. Florence was in and out of hospitals for transfusions every time her skin paled. My mother stopped smiling; my dad became more and more stoic. Our home was always in emotional flux. When Florence started to look pale and the thought of another transfusion became a reality, my parents walked around the house like zombies. Ken and I felt helpless. After a transfusion was completed, we all were able to breathe a sign of relief and enjoy a brief period of happiness.

In late November of 1963, during a visit to the doctor Florence was admitted to Meadowbrook Hospital where she went into a coma a few days later. Since no one in the family drove, we relied on taxicabs to visit her in the hospital. We immediately called for the taxicab. While we were waiting, the phone rang. The voice on the receiver asked to speak to my parents but since they could not speak English, I took the call. The woman's voice on the other end said, "Florence has passed away." I was 15 years old at the time, and couldn't fully comprehend what that meant. The voice at the other end repeated those words and then said more directly, "Florence is dead."

For the first time in my life I was speechless. I didn't know what to say. I felt numb. *No, this couldn't be true. I must be imagining what she said.* But then, I had heard the word "dead" and knew very well what that meant. My eyes swelled and tears flowed. The most difficult task was still to come. *How could I tell Mama and Baba? What possible words could I use?* I, as a teen-ager, had the gut-wrenching responsibility of telling my parents the tragic news with my rusty Chinese vocabulary, which by now had become limited to basic conversation level. *I can't do it. I can't hurt Mama and Baba like this. But if not me, then who?* I was in pain. *How could I tell them? What would I say?* I could feel my voice trembling, my heart beating faster and faster. I finally mustered up the courage and blurted out that Florence had died in the hospital. The overwhelming sadness cannot be described. Mama screamed. Baba cried. The family was devastated. To this day, Mama is unable to visit the Evergreen Cemetery in Brooklyn where Florence is buried. My father weeps every time he makes the annual trip there with my brother.

Added to this loss was the assassination of President John Kennedy a few days later. I was in English class when our teacher told us the news and then turned on the television so we could watch the coverage. At home, as little as my mother knew about politics, I could sense that she felt the loss too, along with the loss of her daughter. To her, President Kennedy was the symbol of this country, the symbol of hope in the country we now considered our home.

We weathered hard times at the laundry. After the death of my sister, Baba took a full time job as a waiter in a Chinese restaurant while Mama immersed herself fully to running the laundry on her own. The Chinese laundry business had slowed down significantly due to the large dry cleaners that had opened up, offering more competitive services for less cost. In addition, the era of polyester created less of a need for shirts to be hand ironed. My parents worked hard to keep the customers they had by providing the best service they could. I remember watching Mama carry out heavy packages for customers who could very well have carried their own. I felt angered by the injustice of it all. "Mama, why can't they carry their own packages? It's too heavy for you," I would say. To this, she was always quick to remind me, "Fay-Jin, in business one must do whatever is necessary to keep the customers – no exceptions."

To be competitive my parents never took a single day off for all the years the laundry was opened. We never took family vacations. When September came around and we were asked in school to share how we spent our summers, Ken and I had little to share. I remember Ken telling the class we went on a vacation trip we had never taken, just to fit in.

On rare occasions, we took day trips such as our trip to Coney Island with Baba. We took the train to Coney Island and walked on the boardwalk near the beach. Baba always wore his black dress shoes wherever he went, which prevented us from walking on the sand. It was a special day and Baba bought a roll of cotton candy for Ken and me to share. I was thrilled to be someplace outside the laundry and in a place that was not just Chinatown.

For a very long time, my parents did not take vacation time to visit their own families in China.

Mama had not been back to China since she left in 1950. Routinely, I would comment, "Mama, Baba, go back to China to see your parents. I can take care of the store during my summers off. I know what needs to be done." Finally, in 1981, 31 years later, they accepted my offer to cover the laundry while they went to China to visit Mama's parents. As a teacher on my summer break, with two young children of my own, I ran the laundry for three weeks in the heat of the summer (and still no air conditioning). I ironed shirts and did whatever it took to operate the laundry during the time my parents were away. I knew that since I had learned what to do over the years that I was the only one they trusted to run the laundry in their absence. It was the very least I could do for all the sacrifices they had made for us. As it turned out, it was a good thing that Mama returned to her village in China that year. The following year, her mother, my maternal Pau-Pau (grandmother), passed away. In some eerie sense, it was as if Pau-Pau had waited for Mama to return before she could leave the earth in peace.

My parents' sacrifice weighed heavily on me as I also tried to be a normal teen-ager. I tried to help as much as I could around the laundry. I always felt guilty, however, when I went out with friends on days in which the store was especially busy. On Saturdays the shirts needed to be labeled and sent out, on Mondays and Tuesdays they needed to be starched, and on Thursdays they returned pressed and needed to be sorted and packaged. It was hard physical labor and I couldn't just leave Mama all by herself even though I wanted very much to be out with my friends. I would work quickly with Mama to do all the chores then rush out to meet my friends. Mama was always amazed at how quickly I would complete the tasks when I wanted to go somewhere.

I also struggled with living up to my parent's expectations. My parents, like the parents of my Chinese friends, always compared me to others. Mama would always say, "Why can't you be like 'Irene' and stay home to study and not go out all the time?" I would tell my parents, "I'm not Irene and don't want to be like Irene. I want to have fun too." I wanted so badly for my parents to see that I was not like anyone else. Even though I knew I should not have raised my voice to my parents, I did on occasions when I really felt I was right. Of course, Mama was quick to remind me that "Good children do not talk back to their parents. Children are not to be heard, especially young girls." And Baba would always respond in his usual "Hmmm – don't talk back to your mother – no good." Mama and Baba never complimented us when we did something well because they believed, as did many other Chinese parents, that positive feedback would jinx the good behavior.

I always knew my parents loved me, even though they didn't openly express it in traditional Western manners. There were rare exceptions. One remains vivid in my mind. Going to Chinatown was always a treat. Every once in a while on Sundays, the family would walk two blocks to the East Williston train station and take the Long Island Railroad into the city. One day it was late and I was tired. We had just come home from Chinatown and had gotten off the train. I started to walk ahead of my parents, across the railroad tracks, carrying grocery packages as I always did, and did not realize another train was coming down in the opposite direction. The horn from the train was honking and my family was screaming. In my catatonic state of fatigue, I heard nothing. What I eventually heard was the sound of a total stranger, an Afri-

*Ginny and Ken as teenagers, 1966*

can American gentleman, who screamed so loud at me that instinctively I ran back toward my parents. My parents both hugged me telling me how happy they were that I was safe. I felt loved and safe. This man had saved my life and to this day, I wish I knew who he was to express my appreciation.

When I was a young girl, Mama gave me a jade necklace that her sister, my Ai-Yee, brought with her when she came to the United States. I understood that she was giving me a mother-daughter heirloom to remember her and our cultural heritage. "Keep it with you always," she said. "The necklace will stay with you, and change with you." She was right. The jade piece changed its translucency, as the stone absorbed my body's oils over the years. What was once a clear green colored stone developed a darker streak of green down the middle. Since the jade was given to me, I have worn it almost every day to remind me that Mama is always with me. One day, one of my students who had long graduated from my class approached me and said, "You must be Ms. Eng. I recognize the jade necklace you always wore when you were my 7th grade teacher."

My parents, particularly Baba, had extremely strict rules for a teenager. This was especially true when it came to boys, a topic that was rarely discussed at home. I remember boldly asking "At what age can I go out on a date?" Mama would either turn a deaf ear or say, "Don't talk about that," and the issue died.

In Junior High School, I developed a crush on a boy who was in one of my classes. Over the course of the year the relationship grew more serious. He became what was referred back then as my steady boyfriend. I wanted to introduce him to my parents but I knew that was totally out of the question for two main reasons. First, relationships with boys were not permitted. And second, he was not of Chinese descent. To have a relationship was already frowned upon, but with someone who was not Chinese was unspeakable. With great frustration, I always wondered, "Why wouldn't they at least meet him and get to know him? If they did, they would see that he is really a very nice person." But that was not going to happen, and I had to do what I needed to do to survive. I ended up meeting him around the corner, away from my parents' sight. Although I justified in my own mind that my parents forced me to sneak around them, there is no denying that I did so with some degree of guilt and envied my friends who were dating with their parents' consent.

Having the approval of my parents was of great importance to me. But, perhaps, what was more important at times was my need to do what I truly felt was the right thing. I was confident that I was making some good decisions at the time and fought hard to have those decisions respected. Most of the time, they were not.

One day while in Chinatown, a boy I was speaking with on the street started to leave and said in passing, "See you later," which was simply a way of saying farewell. My dad immediately asked me, "Who is he? Why is he going to see you later?" It was hard to explain to Baba that the phrase was just a casual, general comment. I always felt as though I were under constant scrutiny when it came to the topic of boyfriends. Over the years, relationships with boys were never part of the family discussions, especially if they were not Chinese Americans. I ended up meeting my friends outside the home.

Similarly, my parents scrutinized the clothes I wore. Baba thought that young women should be conservatively dressed in public. He always commented on my shorts and skirts, indicating they were too short and not appropriate, even though everyone else my age was wearing the same styles. I wanted him to understand that we were not in China; we were in America and things are different. But neither he nor Mama could see the difference.

I rebelled against my parents' restrictions, even

though I always knew they were only doing what they thought was best for me. I had an independent mind and spirit. I fought back continuously and confronted my parents with many challenges throughout my teenage

*Ginny at high school graduation, 1967*

years. So often I thought, "I don't want to live in this house anymore. Mama and Baba are so mean." I threatened to run away from home, but I had no place to go. I resorted to silent disobedience, but realized my parents were happy when I was quiet. My teenage years were difficult years for all of us.

My parents worried about us, particularly their daughter. "In China, children always listened to their parents and never disobeyed. Have we done the right thing bringing them to America?" Mama would often ask Baba. They had made sacrifices primarily to give their children a better life. And they thought the sacrifices would be worthwhile. Similarly, one of our cousins back in China gave up a career as a scientist to come to America working in a sewing factory as a seamstress – all in the hopes of a better life for her next generation.

I had a new jolt of identity crisis in the mid-1960s when our family heard the talk around Chinatown regarding a new amnesty program. The local Chinese newspapers, which Baba read, announced that the U.S. government would pardon anyone who had come to this country as a "paper son," was a military veteran, and lived here for a designated period of time. This

Confession Program was established to acknowledge the role played by veterans of World War II who were tax paying, law-abiding citizens over a significant number of years. Baba saw this as an opportunity to reclaim his real name. With the help of friends, he submitted his paperwork and initiated the process to change his name from Eng Duck Sun to Eng Bing Kuey.

In so doing, Baba never realized the impact this action would have on my citizenship. I quickly learned that my citizenship would become void since I was over eighteen at the time and in the eyes of the law, an adult. My brother was under eighteen and as a minor, was able to retain his citizenship with the processing of Baba's paperwork. I was required to go through the arduous process of applying for citizenship on my own as if I were a new immigrant to this country, waiting the usual five or more years before being granted citizenship – even though I had lived here since I was six years old and spoke the language fluently, and sworn allegiance to this country every day of my life at school.

The period from when I applied for citizenship to when it was granted was an awkward time in my life. I felt as if I were stripped of my identity and my sense of "belonging." *How could I go to sleep a citizen one day and wake up the next morning not a citizen? How could I, a teacher in a school in the United States, tell anyone I was not a U.S. citizen?* No one would ever understand what happened. Finally, five years later, in 1973, I was notified of my new status, and, along with hundreds of others, swore allegiance to the United States of America as a naturalized citizen in a crowded court room in Brooklyn, New York.

# 7

# Outside the Laundry Walls

Freedom. In 1967, I arrived as a freshman at the campus of the University of New York at Cortland, an egress from the laundry into the larger outside world. In the late 1960s students had to abide by dormitory rules related to curfews and visitors. To some people, the rules were too controlling and structured. To me, however, the rules didn't hamper my newfound freedom. My parents were no longer around to tell me what I couldn't do

and what I should be doing. I was not around them to feel guilty about what I wasn't doing around the laundry. It truly was an "out of sight, out of mind" experience for me.

During the previous years when I was in high school, my family and I were continuing to adjust – albeit at different paces – to the American way of life. I embraced the new experiences. I did well in my classes and had many friends. I participated in after-school activities that were initially viewed by my parents as frivolous. I was active in student government, served as treasurer of the Student Council and was Senior Class President. I was also a finalist for prom queen and voted "most likely to succeed" by my senior classmates. Nothing could have been more perfect. On the other hand, my parents grudgingly accepted some (definitely not all) of the practices that were out of the realm of acceptance when they first arrived.

Ken and I left home the same year for college, leaving Mama alone. It was difficult for her to go from the noise, laughter, and the arguments of having us both around to, all of a sudden, the silence of having neither one of us around. For Mama that initial period of separation was one of the most difficult transitions of her life – which surprisingly she acknowledged years later.

As Mama was experiencing empty-nest syndrome, Ken and I had spread our wings into the boundless sky. At college, our transition into American life further accelerated. We both attended New York state schools for financial reasons. Ken decided to attend the University of New York at Stony Brook. I decided to go farther away from home. I chose the University of New York at Cortland and spent four years in training for a career in teaching.

*Ginny during college days*

Change was in the air at college campuses throughout the country in the late 1960s. The turbulence of the period had also reached conservative Cortland. Co-ed dorms were a "first" to happen on our campus, followed by more liberal curfews. Drugs quickly found their way onto our campus, as they were on campuses throughout the nation.

The fervor of the Vietnam War was evident. We, as college students, felt it when the lottery system was in place to decide who would be drafted by number. We were all apprehensive as we waited to see what would happen to our loved ones. I remember thinking of my brother and how relieved I was to learn that his number was high, which meant less of a likelihood he would be drafted. All I could think about was how Mama would have reacted if his number had been low.

Going through four years at Cortland, or any college during the 60s, without ever having experimented with drugs at the time was quite an accomplishment. As a basically contented person, I never felt the need to experiment. I watched my friends wallow in self pity under the influence of drugs and decided it was not for me. I attributed my conviction not to any feat of heroism, or to diminish those who may have experimented, but to my own personal feelings about who I was and what I needed to be fulfilled. The family values that were so deeply ingrained in me gave me the strength to be an active participant in certain aspects of the 60s culture and reject others.

All around me fellow students were changing, myself included. For good or for bad, my traditional ideas about families, relationships and life evolved into a better understanding and acceptance of different family structures, civil rights and race issues, and a desire to explore my identity as an Asian American. I was aware of race riots throughout the country but couldn't fully comprehend the militant nature of those fighting for change.

While I was transformed along with the world around me, my parents never changed. Going home during college breaks was always a walk down memory lane. It was wonderful to see Mama and Baba after having been away. Year after year, my parents were reminders to me that there are parts of me that would, and should, never change. My roots started in the laundry as a Chinese immigrant and that is where my heart will always be. The wings that I found after leaving for college have provided me with the freedom to be "me," but those wings have also been successful in bringing me back home.

# 8

# Wiping the Slate Clean

"Good morning, class. I am Ms. Eng, your new teacher," I said as I smiled proudly at the students who looked back at me. My path from the play classroom under the ironing board to a real classroom had come full circle.

Earlier that year in May 1971, I had received my diploma with a degree in K-12 Mathematics Education. At graduation, I was relieved to know that I had a job in hand in my chosen profession. I was well aware that several of my classmates were having difficulty finding teaching jobs.

Also, I had been nervous about my job search prospects due to my situation at home with parents who are limited English proficient. I had given the school district officials with whom I had interviewed my parents' home number as the contact information. Mama would mention in passing, sometimes days later, "Fay-Jin, by the way, someone called you. I think it was from a school." "Mama, do you know what school? Were they offering me a job?" I would ask and invariably, Mama's response would be, "I don't know." I was frustrated at the possibility that I was losing job opportunities.

Then, I landed an interview with Port Washington Schools district in the north shore of Nassau County. After an extensive interview with one of the system administrators, I left. I started driving up the boulevard when I looked in the rear view mirror and saw a car following me closely and flashing lights to get my attention. I pulled over, believing that I was about to get a ticket. To my pleasant surprise, it was the interviewer I had just met with. "Ms. Eng, I'd like you to come back to the office with me and meet someone who has a vacancy in his school," he said. I did and was then offered a job that day with an annual salary of $8,750.

After graduation, Mama and Baba had a surprise to share with us. "Fay-Jin and Yut-Kew, we just purchased a two family building in Elmhurst, Queens, where the two of you can live," Baba said. "When each of you marry and have families and when we retire, there will be a place for all of us to live together," added Mama. Like many other Chinese parents, their dream was that one day we would all reside together, as was the custom among Chinese families, who, in the old days, lived in a family compound. That never happened. Ken and I shared one apartment for about a year when first entering the workforce while my parents rented out the other two. Then I moved away when I got married and Ken moved out about two years later. My parents moved into the apartment when they retired and have resided there to this day.

In 1971, I met Carl, my husband of 26 years, during a trip to San Francisco between graduation and the start of my new teaching career. I had wanted to see what it was like to live in a community with a significant Asian American population. Growing up, one could count the number of Asian American families in the area in one hand. Carl is a second-generation Asian American who lived in Queens and had more exposure to Asian Americans as a student at Brooklyn Tech High School. Although Carl may have encountered more Asian Americans in school, I grew up with a greater appreciation for being Asian American than he did. Perhaps that was due to the fact that his parents were fluent in speaking English and his family was much more acculturated into mainstream activities.

The following year, 1972, Carl and I married. More than 700 guests attended our wedding celebration, which took place over two days in three different restaurants, two on Saturday and one on Sunday. Guests for Saturday's event were primarily our 100 personal friends and members of Carl's family who were employed in professional jobs. Guests on my side, many of whom worked in laundries, were only able to attend on Sunday when the laundries were closed. According to Chinese traditions, everyone in the family is invited to a wedding, not just the parents. Since both Carl and I were the first to marry in our families, everyone who had ever invited our families to a wedding in the past received an invitation to our wedding.

On the wedding day, as is customary, I was presented with jewelry from the closest relatives. The jewelry was either jade or gold – and of course, if it was gold, it had to be 24 karat gold, anything less was really not considered gold. Twenty-four karat gold is very distinctive in that it is very yellow in color. I remember when I was much younger and given a 24 karat gold necklace and commenting to Mama, "This is so yellow and gaudy. It looks fake and cheap." As I grew older, I came to appreciate the vivid color, and of course, the value.

Carl's interest in becoming a dentist brought us back on campus at the University of Pennsylvania from 1975 to 1979, during which time our children Jennifer and Brian were born. Being parents on a student budget was truly challenging, especially since I had to be home with the children. I recall waiting on line with Jennifer and Brian to submit our application for food stamps and being awarded what was considered a generous monthly food stipend. For approximately a year, we survived on food stamps. We were grateful for any assistance.

After teaching four years in New York, I was in for a surprise when I accepted a job to teach in a suburb of Philadelphia. The school where I was to report for the first day was located in a tough, working-class neighborhood. Walking past a group of students dressed in Hells Angels attire on my way into the school, I heard, "Chink, chink, chink!" The sound of that word evoked such a string of hurt feelings that hit at the core of who I was. It was difficult to hold back the tears, but I did. I would not give these students the satisfaction that they had succeeded in discovering a vulnerable area. Much to my surprise, I saw the same students enter my classroom as my students. But they were not entering through the door; they were coming in through the window. In a firm voice, I told them to climb back out, and come in through the front door of the school building as they were supposed to. I watched the backs of their leather motorcycle jackets with the Hells Angels insignia disappear out of the window. They entered into my classroom again – through the doors. Nothing more was said. We all moved on. As weeks went by the student who gave me the hard time that first day became my strongest allies.

I quickly realized that the students living in this area were simply not accustomed to seeing Asian Pacific Americans. One female student said to me, "I don't know what you are, but you're pretty." To which I replied, "Thanks. I'll consider that a compliment."

After Carl graduated from dental school in 1979, we returned to New York to be near our family and purchased a home in Long Island. Carl was employed as a resident in a nearby hospital and I returned to teaching in Port Washington. We needed child care and my first thought was of my parents who were more than willing to help care for their grandchildren. Every day we would drop Jennifer and Brian off at the laundry and leave for work. When Mama and Baba retired to their home in Queens, the commute became a more challenging one. Every school day, we began the ritual of bringing Jennifer and Brian to my parents in Queens from Long Island where we lived, and then picking them up after work. I would leave the house with the children before 6:00 a.m., compete with rush hour traffic to go into Queens, then go back against more traffic to Long Island, where I worked, and be in front of the classroom by 7:15 a.m.

After work, I would pick up Carl and we would travel out to Queens to get the children. Since the commute back to Long Island would be in rush hour, we generally had dinner that was prepared by Mama before returning home.

I was a busy working mother in suburbia when a school incident involving my daughter Jennifer moved me into social justice activism. Five-year-old at the time, my daughter came home from kindergarten excited. "Mommy, mommy, look!" she said. She took her fingers and pulled up the outer skins of her temples back to elongate her eyes and smiled, happily. I was thunderstruck. I learned that children at school had been making "Asian eyes" gestures at her. Jennifer thought she was getting special treatment, which she was, but not positive treatment. I sat my daughter down, and explained to her that the Asian eyes play was not nice.

After our conversation, I thought to myself, *I have to commit to changing peoples' perception of Asian Pacific Americans. What can I do to make a difference?* I decided to make a commitment to an organization. After researching community organizations, I came across the Long Island chapter of the Organization of Chinese Americans (OCA), a national membership organization engaged in social justice and education work on behalf of Asian Pacific Americans. I became a committed member and stayed involved with local OCA chapters wherever our family moved. Eventually, I took on leadership positions on the national board, the governing Executive Council, and served as its National President twice, each for two consecutive terms. Currently I am serving my fourth term as OCA's National President.

Understanding my identity as an Asian Pacific American was of great interest for me. In the summer of 1981, I decided to return to China and see my only remaining grandparent, my Gung-Gung (maternal grandfather). My parents, concerned about my ability to navigate the country with my limited grasp of the Chinese language, returned with me to Canton. What an experience that was for someone who had not been back to China since the age of 2! I was humbled by what I saw – people working diligently for a few dollars a week in primitive surroundings. The sense of caring for elders was most impressive. Although my Gung-Gung was in need of constant medical care, he remained at home under the watchful eyes of his grand-daughter and her husband. Mama and Baba reminded me that "It's the duty of Lai-Saan and her husband to take care of your Gung-Gung. After all, he was there for them when they were growing up." The belief that life comes full circle was evident. Nursing homes were not a traditional consideration for the elderly in China.

I had come from a country where we make decisions about what wallpaper to put in our posh bathrooms to a country where most families did not have their own toilet. It was a rude awakening. I thought to myself, "How lucky I am to be living in America. We have so much to be thankful for." I was grateful I had the chance to visit China when I did. The following year Gung-Gung passed away.

I would leave teaching, and return to it a third time at Herricks Schools in Searingtown, New York. In the interim, we had our third child, David, in 1982, and moved into a large, 75-year-old home. But before we finished unpacking, we moved again, this time to North Carolina. Carl had just accepted a position in Winston Salem.

In North Carolina, I was in for another culture shock. Having lived in New York for so many years, I was used to living in diverse communities. In Winston Salem our neighborhood was homogeneous. Residents were affluent Whites. Some people were as equally surprised to encounter someone who looked like me and my family. A contractor who came to our house to install linoleum floors remarked, "I've never seen a Chinese person before. Do they all look like you?" I responded jokingly, "Not really. Chinese generally do not have the freckles I have."

I had mixed experiences in North Carolina. On the one hand, we had very nice neighbors and our family was accepted. I attended social teas and learned to enjoy coffee from bone china. On the other hand, interestingly, integration was in place in this area of the south. In Winston Salem, the local school's student population was a majority minority due to "white flight." Many had placed their children in private schools. We felt compelled to transfer Jennifer and Brian out of their home school as well when it was brought to our attention that the KKK might be recruiting from students in the school system.

The landmark Supreme Court case, Brown versus Board of Education, had been decided in 1954, the year I arrived in America and the Chinese Exclusion Act, in place since 1882, was lifted just about a decade ago. But, it was clear to me that even 30 years later, race relations were still a work in progress. Further, America was defining race as a binary Black-White issue. I remember thinking, "What about the rest of us Americans, including Asian Pacific Americans?" I tucked the experience away, but it was not long before I became involved in civil rights issues.

Two years later Carl's career brought us back to New York again. We had come full circle. The market in the mid-1980s had escalated dramatically and we couldn't afford to even buy back our old home. My return to teaching made it possible for us to be a two-income family and purchase a home in Manhasset, 10 minutes away from Ken in Great Neck. A few years later, we moved again. Carl accepted a new job.

Our family made our last move together to Potomac, Maryland in 1990. I capped my teaching career with an education-related position that involved personnel recruitment and management of EEO/equity issues for Montgomery County Public Schools (MCPS). Soon, I was dealing with a full range of race-related issues every day.

As an Asian Pacific American, I was in a unique position to see different viewpoints. I found this vantage point to be helpful when I mediated conflicts between Black and White employees. Black employees felt that, as a minority, I understood the minority perspective, which I did. White employees treated me as if I were White and could understand their views, which I also did. I came to understand that all communities are capable of being discriminatory and discriminated against. It is all a matter of who is in power and has control.

I also handled cases in which cultural competency was critical to understanding employee performance. For example, a female Asian American employee who was very productive and worked very hard was evaluated by her supervisor for not being a good "team player." "I am such a hard worker and produce so much work, I would get a good evaluation if I had a Chinese boss," she complained. I had to point out to her that American standards for job performance are different and it is important that she understand the criteria used in an employee evaluation. Then, I consulted with her supervisor and explained that the employee's model for success in the workplace was culturally influenced. With the new understanding, both parties made a commitment to improve communication and broaden their understanding of each other's expectations.

While employed at MCPS, I established the highly successful Asian Pacific American Parents Network. This model outreach program encouraged the participation of Asian Pacific American parents, resulting in the election of one of the network's initial participants as its countywide PTA president.

It became clear that, with all our moves, I would always gravitate to career choices in the public/education sector. With my children growing up and moving out, I started to accelerate my community involvement in issues that I had grown passionate about over the course of my life.

# 9

# From Board to Board

I was transfixed in a moment as faces around the boardroom turned to me when I made the following comment: "There are so few Asian American faces on television" during a discussion related to minorities on television. At the time, I was serving on the Montgomery Community Television (MCT) board. MCT created local programming for the residents of Montgomery County, Maryland. MCT aired a broad range of shows, including community events, athletic games, senior shows, roundtable talk show among local journalists and religious services to the county's diverse TV viewing audience. MCT provided a quality service, except that there was one problem – very few Asian American faces appeared on the screen.

At that time, Montgomery County was home to approximately 90,000 Asian Pacific Americans (APA), or 11% of the total population in the county. Half of the state's APA population lived in Montgomery County. The population growth had been phenomenal, growing 400% over the last 20 years. Similarly, across the country, APAs were taking the lead as the fastest-growing minority group.

My colleagues on the board challenged me to do something about the situation. I accepted the challenge and together with my producer, Yen Chen, the concept of a TV talk show was born. The first show debuted in 1998 to very positive reviews. *The Gazette,*

Montgomery County's local newspaper, wrote: "To watch as Gong hosts *Ginny's* is to view an original...a down to earth empathy and an exceedingly easy rapport with her guests." The weekly talk show has aired a few times a week, every week, since then. The opening, *"Welcome to* Ginny's ... Where East Meets West...*and a slice of eastern philosophy becomes a part of western thinking. I'm your host Ginny Gong,"* has become a familiar part of the weekly programming on Channel 21. For just about a decade, I have interviewed about 200 people, representing the full spectrum of the Asian Pacific American community, from high level federal officials, including a U.S. Cabinet secretary, war heroes, and civil rights activists, to professors, doctors, business owners, martial artists and actors to anything that is Asian related.

Among the common themes that arose in the show was full acceptance of APAs into American society. I saw this challenge in KAI, an up-and-coming a capella group, whose members are Asian Pacific Americans. They appeared on my show and shared a poignant experience with the viewers which struck a chord with me personally. After the release of their first CD, KAI enjoyed great popularity on the radio waves. DJs often received requests to play their music. KAI's fans often thought KAI's members were Black. They were coming out with a new CD, and had to shoot a cover and were faced with a marketing challenge. They asked themselves, "Should we include a photo of ourselves on the cover? Will our fans enjoy our music differently?" Ultimately, KAI did the photo shoot. CD sales lagged behind their on-air popularity. But KAI members say they have no regrets. "We are proud of our APA heritage."

When I started the show, I wanted TV viewers to become so accustomed to seeing diverse faces on TV

Ginny's ... Where East Meets West *TV show, 1998*

that they would feel an immediate comfort level with people of different backgrounds. Based on my viewers' feedback, progress has been made.

"You are really funny," one viewer told me in passing, apparently surprised that APAs had a sense of humor. Another regular viewer, herself an APA, said, "I'm improving my English and learning about different ethnicities from watching your show."

While media can broadcast positive images, conversely it can also cast harmful negative stereotypes.

In 2007, two DJs from the radio show *The Dog House with JV and Elvis* on WFNY, 92.3 Free FM, in New York City, aired a prank phone call to a Chinese restaurant. They badgered the party on the other line with Asian stereotypes and sexual innuendo for six long minutes. As shock jocks, they made a living from pushing the bounds of decency. There was concern that unless the show was challenged, its listeners would either feel encouraged to copycat the discriminatory behavior or feel validated to have similar attitudes. CBS, the parent company of both shows, was to hear from OCA and many other Asian Pacific American organizations. In response, CBS terminated the show.

I was serving my fourth term as National President of OCA at the time. In recent years, OCA has responded to some other similar shock jock incidents across the country, challenging the insensitivity of such programming. Together with presidents of the four

OCA chapters in the New York area, I met with CBS President and CEO Leslie Moonves to express appreciation to CBS for taking timely, responsible action to terminate the show and the employment of those individuals involved. "We can not guarantee this will not happen again," Moonves told us. "But we can assure you that CBS will take appropriate action if it does."

Not all my work as National President dealt with high profile meetings. Behind the scenes, I was hard at work with the board, staff and volunteers. During my first two terms in 1993 and 1994, I had focused on involvement of the next generation, which included youth programs and leadership development. After a 10-year hiatus, I was recruited to run for National President once again in 2005 and was elected to serve another two terms until the end of 2008. During the two latter terms, OCA reached major milestones. Most significant was the purchase of the new headquarters building in Washington D.C. and the establishment of the OCA National Center. This marked the first permanent presence for the APA community. When I step down as OCA's National President, I will have invested almost half of my life as an advocate dedicated to ensuring a voice for a community that virtually had no voice, and, a community that was often referred to as "invisible."

Sometimes one wonders if our actions as parents have any impact on our children. I realized when my son was in high school that they do. I was truly proud when my youngest son, David, chose to run for President of the Asian American Club when he could have chosen to do something else. He was elected and demonstrated great leadership in that capacity.

I accepted invitations to serve on numerous boards, particularly mainstream boards, believing that people are always more willing to accept ideas and suggestions if they came from someone they were comfortable with. Working from within has been a winning formula for me. I have been able to raise issues and have them considered seriously by my colleagues on the boards. Some of the boards I have had the privilege of participating include: Leadership Montgomery, Governor's Asian Pacific American Advisory Commission, Governor's Advisory Council for New Americans (served as the first chair), Police Chief Advisory Board, MGM Mirage Diversity Council, Montgomery Community Television, The Universities at Shady Grove (vice chair), Arts and Humanities Steering Committee, among others.

Moreover, I have had numerous opportunities to be keynote speaker, panelist, or facilitator of forums and trainings that focused on my passions – youth/ education, diversity/inclusion, the APA community and immigration. It is important for people to see Asian Americans in these visible roles and not just behind computers. I recall a number of occasions whereby a conference attendee, an Asian Pacific American, came up to me and commented on how surprised, and proud, they were to see an Asian Pacific American keynote speaker.

In my professional career, I now serve as the first Asian American appointed by a County Executive to head an agency in Montgomery County. As such, I was in a position to recommend the establishment of the New Americans Welcome Center to help immigrants navigate the complex countywide system of services. Montgomery County Executive, Doug Duncan, embraced the idea and created the Gilchrist Center that serves this purpose. I have found over the years that the work I do in my professional and volunteer orbits often complement each other.

In reflection, I attribute my actions to two very common expressions. "Know thyself" is one that describes the self confidence I have always had in who I am, what I do, and why. I know my strengths, weaknesses, passions, goals and aspirations. I am extremely creative, empathetic and resourceful. I do not hesitate to speak up for causes and issues I believe in and am always conscious of when, where and how that should be done. I realize that the messenger is critical to the message, and that is what is most important. I have always been an advocate for the downtrodden and the weak in our social system. Growing up as I did has made me aware of the differences that exist in our society. I believe there are inequities in the way people are treated just because they are different in race, gender and so on and I am saddened by this reality. But, I also believe that we can create our own destiny and I am always optimistic about that.

"Seek and ye shall find" is another expression that guides my actions and reminds me of how I should be looking at situations I am presented with. If I look for discrimination, I will find it. If I look for favoritism, I will find it. And if I look for open doors of opportunity, I will find those as well. I have chosen to see the "glass half full" and not "half empty." As my son, Brian, always reminds me, "It's all good, mom."

Once, I was a little girl who lived within the confines of a laundry with big dreams of life on the outside. It seems that the little girl managed to live her dreams. I have the good fortune of raising three children, developing a career in education, administration, and the public sector, and assuming leadership roles on several nonprofit and corporate boards. I

*Ginny, Baba, Mama and Ken, 2005*

make commitments to causes I have always believed in. I owe a significant debt to my parents who shaped my thinking and influenced my actions in the hearth of the Chinese Hand Laundry. Mama and Baba are healthy seniors living in their home in Elmhurst, Queens. They say little about the life meanderings I've taken from the laundry, with one exception.

After reading about some of my accomplishments in the Chinese newspaper, Baba asked, "Ginny, why didn't you use your maiden Chinese name? How

will people know you are related to us?" Translation:
He is proud.

# EPILOGUE

*I have come to see the world as a much bigger place – beyond the confines of a laundry and beyond the thinking of America as a white community. I have witnessed inequities in American society that are both obvious and subtle, as well as sincere efforts to equalize the playing field. Over the last 35 years, I have met many influential people who have dedicated much personal energy to making a difference in this world. And I have been fortunate to have had the opportunity to have played a role in this movement.*

*The many moves in my life have shaped my perspectives and affected my actions. I have been afforded many opportunities to serve on boards that are both policymaking and advisory. My commitment to community service and to causes I am passionate about has enabled me to bring about changes in local, state, and national arenas.*

*Jennifer, Ginny, Brian, and David*

*I have changed in so many ways — ironing boards replaced by chalk boards, and finally corporate and community boards; the narrow parochial view of a tightly knit immigrant family to a broader, more liberal view of the "family of man" in general.*

*The laundry no longer exists on Hillside Avenue but the memories of time spent there remain as vivid as ever. Whatever my perspectives, attitudes, or actions, I know they were rooted during those formative years spent behind the ironing board...*

# Homa & Sekey Books Titles on China

**September's Fable: A Novel**
By Zhang Wei. Trans. by Terrence Russell & Shawn X. Ye
Order No 1050, ISBN-10: 1931907463, ISBN-13: 9781931907460
Paperback, 6 x 9, 495p, 2007, $29.95, Fiction

*September's Fable* tells the story of the rise and fall of a Chinese coastal village through its difficult formation, hard existence and inevitable disintegration. Spanning approximately sixty years, the novel is a rich and intriguing tapestry of life and death in rural China. Somewhat in the tradition of William Faulkner and Gabriel García Márquez, September's Fable weaves history, politics, and folklore close together to bring an enchanting way of storytelling that dexterously touches on such universal themes as love and hate, war and revolution, city and country, the noble and the ugly, and, more importantly, the inevitability of the old superseded by the new and young.

**Journey across the Four Seas: A Chinese Woman's Search for Home** By Veronica Li
Order No: 1047, ISBN: 1931907439, Paperback, 6 x 9, 298p, 2007, $14.95, Nonfiction/Memoir

This is a true and touching story of one Chinese woman's search for home. It is also an inspiring book about human yearning for a better life. To escape poverty, Flora Li fought her way through the education system and became one of the few women to get into the prestigious Hong Kong University. Throughout her migrations, from Shanghai to Nanking to Hong Kong to Bangkok to Taipei and finally across the four seas to the U.S., Flora kept her sight on one goal—providing her children with the best possible education.

**The Holy Spark: Rogel and the Goddess of Liberty**
By Yu Li, Trans. by Haiyan Chen & Xianfeng Mu
Order No 1046, ISBN 1931907420, Hardcover, 6 x 9, 260p, 2006, $16.99, Fiction

"*The Holy Spark* is a splendid novel in the great tradition of *Alice in Wonderland, The Wonderful Wizard of Oz,* and *The Chronicles of Narnia.* It is perfect for young readers and will keep them highly entertained for hours."
— **Barry Moreno, historian and author, Statue of Liberty & Ellis Island Museum**

# Homa & Sekey Books Titles on China

**The Haier Way: The Making of a Chinese Business Leader and a Global Brand** By Jeannie J. Yi, PhD & Shawn X. Ye, MBA
Order No 1009, ISBN: 1-931907-01-3, Hardcover, Business, $24.95

Haier is the largest consumer appliance maker in China. The book traces the appliance giant's path to success, from its early bleak years to becoming the world's 5th largest household appliance manufacturer. The book explains how Haier excelled in quality, service, technology innovation, a global vision and a management style that is a blend of Jack Welch of "GE" and Confucius of ancient China.

I enjoyed reading through it – A great story! Haier is certainly an impressive company.

— **Jack Welch**, former GE Chairman and CEO

**China's Generation Y:**
**Understanding the Future Leaders of the World's Next Superpower**
By Michael Stanat, United Nations International School
Order No 1029, ISBN 1931907250, Hardcover, 6 x 9, 222 pp., $24.95
Order No 1040, ISBN 1931907323, Paperback, 6 x 9, 222 pp., $17.95
Contemporary Affairs, 2006

Based upon interviews and surveys conducted in Shanghai by the author, this is the first English book to look into all aspects of China's young generation — their life styles, relationships with family and society, views, dreams and development... *China's Generation Y* provides a rare glimpse into the lives and minds of today's youth and tomorrow's leaders, showing Western readers who they are, how they got there, and where they are headed.

**Paintings by Xu Jin: Tradition and Innovation in Chinese Fine Brushwork.** Preface by Prof. Robert E. Harrist, Jr., Columbia University, Order No 1028, ISBN 1931907234, Hardcover, 10½ x 10½, 128pp., color illustrations throughout, $39.50, Art

This book brings together over seventy Chinese fine brushwork paintings by Xu Jin, including figures, landscapes, animals, flowers and birds. Drawing on sources in earlier art and traditional iconography, Xu Jin's paintings are characterized by stylish composition, impressive colors, and fine lines. They not only demonstrate a natural integration of verse, calligraphy, painting and seal, but also a fine combination of Chinese and Western painting skills.

# Homa & Sekey Books Titles on China

**Willow Leaf, Maple Leaf: A Novel of Immigration Blues**
By David Ke, PhD, Order No 1036, ISBN: 1931907242, 5 ½ x 8 ½,
Paperback, 2006, 203 pp., $16.95 Fiction/Asian-American Studies

Willow Leaf is a dazzlingly beautiful Chinese woman who is smuggled
to Canada. While working at a sweatshop and at a massage parlor—and
through several extramarital affairs—she learns that survival in a different country might mean a compromise of morals. Eventually, she finds
new wealth and new love with an elderly man and has her own successful business. But can Willow Leaf truly leave her love for her family and
China behind?

**Flower Terror: Suffocating Stories of China** by Pu Ning
ISBN 0-9665421-0-X, Fiction, Paperback, $13.95

"The stories in this work are well written." **– Library Journal**

Acclaimed Chinese writer eloquently describes the oppression of
intellectuals in his country between 1950s and 1970s in these twelve
autobiographical novellas and short stories. Many of the stories are so
shocking and heart-wrenching that one cannot but feel suffocated.

**The Peony Pavilion: A Novel** by Xiaoping Yen, PhD
ISBN 0-9665421-2-6, Fiction, Paperback, $16.95

"A window into the Chinese literary imagination." **– Publishers Weekly**

A sixteen-year-old girl visits a forbidden garden and falls in love with a
young man she meets in a dream. She has an affair with her dream-lover
and dies longing for him. After her death, her unflagging spirit continues
to wait for her dream-lover. Does her lover really exist? Can a youthful
love born of a garden dream ever blossom? The novel is based on a
sixteenth-century Chinese opera written by Tang Xianzu, "the
Shakespeare of China."

**Butterfly Lovers: A Tale of the Chinese Romeo and Juliet**
By Fan Dai, PhD, ISBN 0-9665421-4-2, Fiction, Paperback, $16.95

"An engaging, compelling, deeply moving, highly recommended and
rewarding novel." **– Midwest Books Review**

A beautiful girl disguises herself as a man and lives under one roof with
a young male scholar for three years without revealing her true identity.
They become sworn brothers, soul mates and lovers. In a world in which
marriage is determined by social status and arranged by parents, what is
their inescapable fate?

# Homa & Sekey Books Titles on China

**The Dream of the Red Chamber: An Allegory of Love**
By Jeannie Jinsheng Yi, PhD, ISBN: 0-9665421-7-7, Hardcover
Asian Studies/Literary Criticism, $49.95

Although dreams have been studied in great depth about this most influential classic Chinese fiction, the study of all the dreams as a sequence and in relation to their structural functions in the allegory is undertaken here for the first time.

**Always Bright: Paintings by American Chinese Artists 1970-1999**
Edited by Xue Jian Xin et al.
ISBN 0-9665421-3-4, Art, Hardcover, $49.95

"An important, groundbreaking, seminal work." –**Midwest Book Review**

A selection of paintings by eighty acclaimed American Chinese artists in the late 20<sup>th</sup> century, *Always Bright* is the first of its kind in English publication. The album falls into three categories: oil painting, Chinese painting and other media painting. It also offers profiles of the artists and information on their professional accomplishment.

**Always Bright, Vol. II: Paintings by Chinese American Artists**
Edited by Eugene Wang, Harvard Univ., et al.
ISBN: 0-9665421-6-9, Art, Hardcover, $50.00

A sequel to the above, the book includes artworks of ninety-two artists in oil painting, Chinese painting, watercolor painting, and other media such as mixed media, acrylic, pastel, pen and pencil, etc. The book also provides information on the artists and their professional accomplishment. Artists included come from different backgrounds, use different media and belong to different schools. Some of them enjoy international fame while others are enterprising young men and women who are more impressionable to novelty and singularity.

**Musical Qigong: Ancient Chinese Healing Art from a Modern Master**
By Shen Wu, ISBN: 0-9665421-5-0, Health, Paperback, $14.95

Musical Qigong is a special healing energy therapy that combines two ancient Chinese traditions-healing music and Qigong. This guide contains two complete sets of exercises with photo illustrations and discusses how musical Qigong is related to the five elements in the ancient Chinese concept of the universe - metal, wood, water, fire, and earth.

# Homa & Sekey Books Titles on China

**Ink Paintings by Gao Xingjian, the Nobel Prize Winner**
ISBN: 1-931907-03-X, Hardcover, Art, $34.95

An extraordinary art book by the Nobel Prize Winner for Literature in 2000, this volume brings together over sixty ink paintings by Gao Xingjian that are characteristic of his philosophy and painting style. Gao believes that the world cannot be explained, and the images in his paintings reveal the black-and-white inner world that underlies the complexity of human existence. People admire his meditative images and evocative atmosphere by which Gao intends his viewers to visualize the human conditions in extremity.

**Splendor of Tibet: The Potala Palace, Jewel of the Himalayas**
By Phuntsok Namgyal, ISBN: 1-931907-02-1, Hardcover,
Art/Architecture, $39.95

A magnificent and spectacular photographic book about the Potala Palace, the palace of the Dalai Lamas and the world's highest and largest castle palace. Over 150 rare and extraordinary color photographs of the Potala Palace are showcased in the book, including murals, thang-ka paintings, stupa-tombs of the Dalai Lamas, Buddhist statues and scriptures, porcelain vessels, enamel work, jade ware, brocade, Dalai Lamas' seals, and palace exteriors.

**Breaking Grounds: The Journal of a Top Chinese Woman Manager in Retail** by Bingxin Hu, Preface by Louis B. Barnes, Harvard Business School, ISBN: 1-931907-15-3, 256pp, Hardcover, Business, $24.95

The book records the experience of a Chinese business woman who pioneered and succeeded in modernizing the aging Chinese retail business. Based on her years of business experience, the author recounts the turmoil, clashes of concepts and behind-the-scene decisions in the Chinese retail business, as well as psychological shocks, emotional perplexes, and intellectual apprehension she had gone through.

## www.homabooks.com

**ORDERING INFORMATION: U.S.:** $5.00 for the first item, $1.50 for each additional item. **Outside U.S.:** $12.00 for the first item, $6.00 for each additional item. All major credit cards accepted. You may also send a check or money order in U.S. fund (payable to Homa & Sekey Books) to: Orders Department, Homa & Sekey Books, P. O. Box 103, Dumont, NJ 07628 U.S.A. Tel: 800-870-HOMA; 201-261-8810. Fax: 201-384-6055; 201-261-8890. Email: info@homabooks.com

# Homa & Sekey Books Titles on Korea (1)

**East and West: Fusion of Horizons**
By Kwang-Sae Lee, Kent State University
ISBN 1931907269, Order No 1030, 6 x 9, Hardcover, $59.95, £35.00
ISBN 1931907331, Order No 1041, 6 x 9, Paperback, $34.95, £22.00
**Philosophy/Culture/Comparative Studies**, 2006, xii, 522pp

**A Topography of Confucian Discourse: Politico-philosophical
Reflections on Confucian Discourse since Modernity**
By Lee Seung-hwan, Korea University
ISBN 1931907277, Order No 1031, 6 x 9, Hardcover, $49.95, £30.00
ISBN 193190734X, Order No 1042, 6 x 9, Paperback, $29.95, £19.00
**History/Culture/Philosophy**, 2006, xii, 260pp

**Developmental Dictatorship and the Park Chung-hee Era:
The Shaping of Modernity in the Republic of Korea**
Edited by Lee Byeong-cheon, Kangwon National University
ISBN 1931907285, Order No 1032, 6 x 9, Hardcover, $54.95, £32.00
ISBN 1931907358, Order No 1043, 6 x 9, Paperback, $32.95, £20.00
**History/Politics**, 2006, xviii, 384pp

**The Gwangju Uprising: The Pivotal Democratic Movement
That Changed the History of Modern Korea**
By Choi Jungwoon, Seoul National University
ISBN 1931907293, Order No 1033, 6 x 9, Hardcover, $49.95, £31.00
ISBN 1931907366, Order No 1044, 6 x 9, Paperback, $29.95, £19.00
**History/Politics**, 2006, xx, 326pp

**The Land of Scholars:
Two Thousand Years of Korean Confucianism**
By Kang Jae-eun
ISBN 1931907307, Order No 1034, 6 x 9, Hardcover, $59.95, £35.00
ISBN 1931907374, Order No 1045, 6 x 9, Paperback, $34.95, £22.00
**History/Culture/Philosophy**, 2006, xxx, 516pp

**Korea's Pastimes and Customs: A Social History**
By Lee E-Wha. 16 pages of color photos. B&W illustrations throughout.
ISBN 1931907382, Order No 1035, 6 x 9, Paperback, $29.95, £21.00
**History/Culture**, 2006, x, 264pp

# Homa & Sekey Books Titles on Korea (2)

**A Love Song for the Earnest: Selected Poems of Shin Kyungrim**
ISBN: 1931907390, Order No 1037, 5 ½ x 8 ½, Paperback, xxiv, 72pp
**Poetry,** $11.95, 2006

**Cracking the Shell: Three Korean Ecopoets**
By Seungho Choi, Chiha Kim, and Hyonjong Chong
ISBN: 1931907404, Order No 1038, 5 ½ x 8 ½, Paperback, xxviii, 108pp
**Poetry,** $12.95, 2006

**Sunrise over the East Sea: Selected Poems of Park Hi-jin**
ISBN: 1931907412, Order No 1039, 5 ½ x 8 ½, Paperback, xiv, 124pp
**Poetry,** $10.95, 2006

**Fragrance of Poetry: Korean-American Literature.**
Ed. by Yearn Hong Choi, Ph.D., 5 ½ x 8 ½, Paperback, 108pp
ISBN: 1931907226, Order No. 1027, **Poetry,** $13.95, 2005

**A Floating City on the Water: A Novel** by Jang-Soon Sohn
ISBN: 1931907188, Order No: 1025, 5½ x 8½, Paperback, 178pp
**Fiction,** $14.95, 2005

**Korean Drama Under Japanese Occupation:**
**Plays by Ch'i-jin Yu & Man-sik Ch'ae,** 5½ x 8½, Paperback, x, 178pp
ISBN: 193190717X, Order No: 1026, **Drama,** $16.95, 2004

**The Curse of Kim's Daughters: A Novel** By Park Kyong-ni
ISBN: 1931907102, Order No: 1018, 5½ x 8½, Paperback, 299pp
**Fiction,** $18.95, 2004

**I Want to Hijack an Airplane: Selected Poems of Kim Seung-Hee**
ISBN: 1931907137, Order No: 1021, 5½ x 8½, Paperback, xiv, 188pp
**Poetry,** $15.95, 2004

**Flowers in the Toilet Bowl: Selected Poems of Choi Seungho**
ISBN: 1931907110, Order No: 1022, 5½ x 8½, Paperback, xxvi, 73pp
**Poetry,** $12.95, 2004

**Drawing Lines: Selected Poems of Moon Dok-su**
ISBN: 1931907129, Order No: 1023, 5½ x 8½, Paperback, xvi, 82pp
**Poetry,** $11.95, 2004

**What the Spider Said: Poems of Chang Soo Ko**
ISBN: 1931907145, Order No: 1024, 5½ x 8½
Paperback, xii, 74pp, **Poetry,** $10.95, 2004

**Surfacing Sadness:**
**A Centennial of Korean-American Literature 1903-2003**
Ed. by Yearn Hong Choi, Ph.D & Haeng Ja Kim
ISBN: 1931907099, Order No: 1017, 6 x 9, Hardcover, xxvi,
216pp, **Asian-American Studies/Literature,** $25.00, 2003

**Father and Son: A Novel** by Han Sung-won,
ISBN: 1931907048, Order No: 1010, 5½ x 8½, Paperback, 285pp,
2002, **Fiction,** $17.95

**Reflections on a Mask: Two Novellas** by Ch'oe In-hun.
ISBN: 1931907056, Order No: 1011, 5½ x 8½, Paperback, 258pp,
2002, **Fiction,** $16.95

**Unspoken Voices: Selected Short Stories by Korean Women**
**Writers** By Park Kyong-ni, et al.
ISBN: 1931907064, Order No: 1012, 5½ x 8½, Paperback, 266pp,
2002, **Fiction,** $16.95

**The General's Beard: Two Novellas** by Lee Oyoung,
ISBN: 1931907072, Order No: 1013, 5½ x 8½, Paperback, 182pp,
2002, **Fiction,** $14.95

**Farmers: A Novel** by Lee Mu-young,
ISBN: 1931907080, Order No: 1014, 5½ x 8½, Paperback, 216pp,
2002, **Fiction,** $15.95

## www.homabooks.com

**Ordering Information: Within U.S.:** $5.00 for the first item, $1.50 for each additional item. **Outside U.S.:** $12.00 for the first item, $6.00 for each additional item. All major credit cards accepted. You may also send a check or money order in U.S. fund (payable to Homa & Sekey Books) to: Orders Department, Homa & Sekey Books, P. O. Box 103, Dumont, NJ 07628 U.S.A. Tel: 800-870-HOMA, 201-261-8810; Fax: 201-261-8890, 201-384-6055; Email: info@homabooks.com